Table of Contents

I0008355

About the Book

This comprehensive guide to building a successful CTI program and thoroughly explores the fundamentals of CTI, including various intelligence requirements, sources of information, and techniques for analysis and dissemination. The book provides valuable insights and practical guidance based on real-world case studies to help organizations effectively respond to cyber threats.

The book covers different forms of CTI, such as technical intelligence, open-source intelligence, and human intelligence, providing a comprehensive understanding of the threats organizations face. It also covers the sources of CTI, such as threat intelligence feeds, security alerts, and incident reports, along with techniques for analyzing and disseminating this information to relevant stakeholders.

In addition to theoretical aspects, the book guides readers through the practical aspects of implementing a CTI program, including developing processes, selecting tools, and creating a dedicated CTI team. These reasonable steps are crucial for establishing a successful CTI program.

Whether readers aim to improve their organization's CTI capabilities or seek to understand the field, this book equips them with the necessary knowledge and skills to build and maintain a robust CTI program. With the constantly growing threat landscape, having a comprehensive CTI program has never been more critical, and this book provides the essential guide to do so.

About the Author

Robert possesses extensive knowledge and experience in developing, managing, and executing successful CTI programs, with expertise in intelligence gathering, risk management, fraud prevention and mitigation, as well as the design and automation of security processes. His commitment to remaining up to date with the latest developments and best practices is evidenced by his professional certifications.

As a CTI professional, Robert provides customized CTI solutions to meet the unique security needs of each organization. His diverse sector experience and CTI expertise have given him a broad understanding of the specific cyber threats faced by each industry, making him an asset for any organization looking to enhance their cybersecurity defenses.
In summary, Robert is a highly regarded and accomplished CTI expert with extensive experience and knowledge. He is an indispensable resource for organizations seeking to defend against emerging cyber threats and is well-equipped to lead the development and management of effective CTI programs.

Chapter #1 – Introduction to Cyber-Threat Intelligence (CTI)

Introduction

Cyber Threat Intelligence (CTI) is a critical component of a comprehensive security strategy, designed to gather and analyze both internal and external data to identify potential threats that could negatively impact an organization. CTI enables organizations to make proactive, informed decisions to improve their defensive posture against malicious actors. This is achieved by conducting structured assessments and analyses of potential threats and providing actionable intelligence products to detect, discover, and neutralize potential threats.

The intelligence products offered by CTI include strategic, tactical, technical, and operational intelligence that various internal teams and security tools can consume. Several high-profile vulnerabilities have been exploited in recent years, such as the log4J security hole, the SolarWinds zero-day attack, and the Okta breach. If present in an organization's environment, these vulnerabilities can lead to significant harm, including loss of control over systems, exfiltration of sensitive data, or ransomware deployment in worst-case scenarios.

As a cyber security professional, it is crucial to stay ahead of emerging cyber threats; that is where a well-designed CTI program comes into play. A successful CTI program leverages existing internal sources. It incorporates a proactive component to threat modeling, detection, and response efforts, allowing organizations to maintain a strong defense against potential cyber threats.

It is important to remember that all organizations are unique in size, capabilities, and budget. Hence, there is no one-size-fits-all solution for cyber threat intelligence. While intelligence aggregation and correlation tools can be helpful, they should only be implemented if they align with specific intelligence requirements, use cases, or internal needs. CTI programs can be cost-effective and streamlined to meet the operational intelligence objectives of the organization.

Course Objectives

This book aims to empower you with the knowledge and skills required to establish and effectively implement a Cyber Threat Intelligence (CTI) program within your organization. The book is packed with real-life examples, case studies, and hands-on exercises that will help you grasp the fundamental concepts of CTI and apply them in practice. By the end of this course, you will have a deep understanding of the critical elements of CTI and the ability to use this knowledge to stay ahead of cyber threats.

We will delve into the fundamentals of CTI, emphasizing the importance of a solid understanding of these concepts. This includes explaining the difference between CTI and other forms of intelligence. You will also be presented with examples of various cyber threats organizations face and learn how CTI can be used as a proactive defense mechanism. The goal is to equip you with the knowledge and experience needed to make informed decisions when building and operationalizing your organization's CTI program.

Throughout this course, we will cover topics such as:

- **Establishing a CTI program:** The process of setting up a CTI program, including how to align it with the organization's overall security strategy. We will also provide examples of different types of CTI programs and the benefits they can provide to an organization.

- **Intelligence requirements:** Identifying and prioritizing the information an organization needs to defend against cyber threats effectively. We will also provide examples of different intelligence collection methods and tools used to support the CTI process.

- **Tools and technologies:** Discuss the tools and technologies used to automate CTI operations, such as intelligence collection and analysis, threat detection, and incident response. We will also provide examples of different tools and their features and functionalities.

- **Actionable intelligence:** Discuss how to produce intelligence products that can be integrated and distributed with various teams, stakeholders, and other tools to support decision-making and incident response. This book will also provide examples of different intelligence products and how they are used to defend against cyber threats.

- **Courses-of-Action:** Discuss the different courses of action taken to defend against threats that have the potential to impact the organization negatively. We will also provide examples of different types of threats and how CTI can be used to defend against them.

- **Metrics:** Discuss how to produce critical operational performance metrics highlighting the activities and efficiency of the CTI team. We will also provide examples of different metrics and how they are used to evaluate the effectiveness of a CTI program. It's important to note that each organization is unique in terms of size, capabilities, and budget, so there is no one-size-fits-all solution when it comes to CTI. While intelligence aggregation and correlation tools can be useful, they are only necessary if they meet an organization's intelligence requirements, use cases, or other internal needs.

This comprehensive course is designed to equip you with the essential knowledge and practical skills required to effectively establish and implement a Cyber Threat Intelligence (CTI) program within your organization. With this program in place, your organization will be better equipped to anticipate and mitigate potential cyber threats.

It is important to note that this course focuses solely on the setup, operation, and maintenance of a CTI program. It does not delve into advanced analytical or investigative techniques.

Chapter Objectives

By the end of this chapter, you will be familiar with the core concepts and terminology of cyber threat intelligence, such as intelligence requirements, courses of action, the kill chain, threat con, traffic light protocol, and the intelligence lifecycle. Other topics that will be discussed are the advantages of cyber threat intelligence and how it can support an organization's security posture. We'll also distinguish the objectives and motivations of various adversaries that may target your organization. This understanding is essential for creating effective intelligence collection and analysis plans.

Upon completion of this course, participants will be able to:
- Discuss the fundamental concepts of CTI.
- Outline the steps required to establish a CTI program.
- Create intelligence requirements in support of CTI processes.
- Understand critical tools and technologies used to automate CTI operations.
- Produce actionable intelligence products that can be integrated and distributed with various teams, stakeholders, and other tools.
- Identify and implement appropriate courses of action to defend against threats that have the potential to impact the organization negatively.
- Produce critical operational performance metrics highlighting the activities and efficiency of the CTI team.

When establishing a cyber threat intelligence program, you need to develop clear goals and objectives for the program. This will be followed by identifying relevant threats, intelligence requirements, intelligence sources, and courses of action needed to defend against emerging cyber threats. The CTI program must also include a feedback loop to ensure that the intellect is used effectively and to adjust as necessary. It should also have regular reporting and communication with key stakeholders to inform them of the program's progress and any significant findings.

The below process flow summarizes the stages we will take throughout this book to establish your CTI Program.

Discovery	• Document physical and digital assets used within the organization. • Document Supply Chain, vendors and service providers. • Identify keywords, terms & phrases for monitoring • Identify internal data logs and sources
Risk assessment and threat modelling	• Determine the risks and threats associated with corporate assets. • Model high-level threat scenarios that can impact your organization. • Categorize threat scenarios to support the development of intelligence requirements and/or use cases.
Intelligence requirements	• Leverage discovery information to determine what threats scenarios in scope. • Identify applicable sources for intelligence data. • Determine products and services the CTI team can produce to mitigate cyber threats and reduce risk. • Establish Communication Plans and SLAs
Intelligence tools	• Determine tools to collect, store, & process data. • Understand how various intelligence tools can integrate with each other as well as other security tools, or data sources. • Determine technical dependencies to support CTI tools.
Operational metrics and reporting	• Measure performance of the overall CTI program • Provide insight into the overall threat landscape. • Identify operational metrics and reporting to measure performance and effectiveness of the CTI team and their Courses-of-Action. • Determine required data and where to collect this.
Executive and stakeholder buy-in	• Present the business case for a Threat Intelligence Program. • Describe what a CTI Program can do for the organization. • Obtain strategic direction, approval and funding.

These stages will be discussed in more detail below.

Discovery

The discovery phase is critical for any organization to understand and identify its physical and digital assets and any supply-chain dependencies and vendors or service providers. Cybersecurity professionals must also be aware of the potential reputational harm resulting from a cyber-attack. As such, it is essential to have a thorough understanding of the organization's data and systems and security capabilities to detect and respond to any potential threats.

Cybersecurity professionals play a vital role in this process, as during the discovery phase, they are responsible for identifying internal data logs and sources, documenting, and identifying sensitive assets or intellectual property that may be vulnerable to cyber threats, and essential keywords, terms, and phrases used for intelligence requirement monitoring.

Threat Modelling

To effectively protect an organization's assets, it is crucial for cybersecurity professionals to have a thorough understanding of the potential risks and threats. This includes identifying and categorizing threat modeling scenarios that could impact the organization, such as cyber-attacks, data breaches, and malware infections.

Cybersecurity professionals use various methods to determine these threat scenarios through different threat modeling and assessment techniques. This is to help identify potential weaknesses in an organization's systems and networks and the likelihood and potential impact of a successful attack. Once potential threat scenarios have been established and categorized, cybersecurity professionals can develop intelligence requirements and use cases to protect the organization's assets.

Intelligence Requirements

Organizations must establish a comprehensive cyber security intelligence program to protect their systems and networks from cyber threats effectively. The scope of this program should include the specific threat scenarios being monitored for and the ability to assess the impact of a cyber-attack on their systems and networks, including evaluating the risk to sensitive data and systems and understanding the financial, reputational, and regulatory consequences of a breach. The intelligence requirements vary based on the unique characteristics of each organization, such as industry, size, and infrastructure complexity.

A dedicated team of cyber security experts is crucial for maintaining a robust cyber security intelligence program. These professionals must have the necessary skills and expertise to gather, analyze, and interpret threat intelligence from various sources. They must also effectively communicate this information to relevant stakeholders within the organization. In addition to a dedicated team, clear communication plans and service level agreements (SLAs) are essential for ensuring that the intelligence produced by the program is delivered to stakeholders in a timely and actionable manner. These SLAs should outline the expectations and responsibilities of both the intelligence team and stakeholders, and they should be reviewed and updated regularly to ensure they remain effective and relevant.

Intelligence Tools

Cybersecurity professionals must utilize intelligence tools to effectively protect their systems and data from threats. These tools help to collect, store, and process cyber threat intelligence data and integrate it with other devices and data sources to provide a comprehensive security solution. Using tracking and correlation tools helps enrich the information gathered and provides valuable insights into the security landscape.

Understanding technical dependencies are also essential in the field of cyber security. By knowing how their tools and applications interconnect and rely on each other, professionals can identify and address potential vulnerabilities and ensure that their security solutions provide the highest protection level. Staying up to date on the latest tools and techniques is crucial for cybersecurity professionals to stay ahead of the latest threats and vulnerabilities.

Metrics and Reporting

Operational metrics and reporting are essential aspects of a successful Cyber Threat Intelligence (CTI) program. The focus of operational metrics and reporting is to measure the performance of the CTI program, provide insight into the overall threat landscape, and determine the effectiveness of the CTI team's actions. It is necessary to identify the operational metrics and reports used to measure performance and choose the data required to generate these metrics.

Operational metrics and reporting can include data from different tools, ticketing systems, and logging systems used during the operating period. This data can extract meaningful metrics and generate reports for executives and stakeholders, including charts, graphs, and various types of reports such as word documents, PDFs, or PowerPoint presentations. The data and metrics are extracted using intelligence tools, and meaningful reports will be generated for executives and stakeholders.

Executive and Stakeholder Buy-in

Securing buy-in from executives and stakeholders is critical for the success of the Cyber Threat Intelligence (CTI) program. In this phase, the focus will be on presenting the CTI program's business case and showcasing the benefits it can bring to the organization.

To effectively communicate the value of the CTI program, it is crucial to gather and present key concepts and activities from previous phases. This includes defining intelligence requirements and use cases, identifying data sources, and developing operational metrics and reporting. The information should be presented clearly and concisely, highlighting the CTI program's key benefits.

Additionally, obtaining the necessary funding, budget, hardware, and software servers are essential for the CTI program's success. It is vital to involve executives and stakeholders in the planning process, seeking their strategic direction on the program's focus and desired outcomes. Tailoring the CTI program to meet the organization's specific needs and gaining buy-in from stakeholders and executives will ensure a more successful implementation.

What makes a successful Cyber Threat Intelligence Program

Integration across Security Teams

A well-integrated Cyber Threat Intelligence (CTI) team can benefit an organization significantly. CTI teams are responsible for gathering, analyzing, and disseminating information about potential cyber threats to the organization. A well-integrated CTI team ensures that this information is effectively shared with the appropriate organizational stakeholders, allowing them to make informed decisions and take proper actions to protect the organization from cyber threats.

One of the key benefits of a well-integrated CTI team is improved threat detection and response. The CTI team monitors the threat landscape and identifies potential threats to the organization. By integrating the CTI team throughout the organization, this information can be shared with other groups, allowing them to respond to potential threats quickly and effectively. Doing so can help minimize a cyber-attack impact on the organization.

Another benefit of a well-integrated CTI team is improved incident management. CTI teams can provide valuable information to incident response teams, such as the tactics, techniques, and procedures (TTPs) used by attackers and indicators of compromise (IOCs). This information allows the CTI team to effectively manage and respond to incidents, allowing the organization to contain and mitigate the cyber-attack impact quickly.

A well-integrated CTI team improves the organization's overall security posture. CTI teams can provide valuable information to other groups, such as the security operations center (SOC) and the security engineering team, allowing them to improve the organization's security controls and processes. This can help to proactively prevent cyber-attacks and reduce the overall risk to the organization.

In addition, a CTI team can support the organization's ability to make informed decisions regarding security. By providing valuable information to executive management, such as the overall threat landscape and the organization's risks. This information supports informed decisions about allocating resources and where security efforts should be focused.

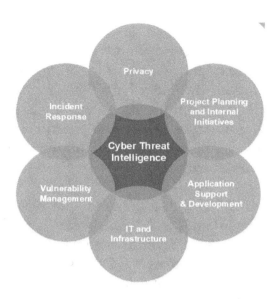

- **Privacy:** Identify the disclosure or potential sale of sensitive information from affected organizations that have recently experienced a breach or compromised.

- **Incident Response:** In an incident, breach, or compromise affecting organizations (directly or indirectly), Threat Intelligence can provide support through in-depth data enrichment based on the artifacts and information identified.

- **Vulnerability Management:** Monitor for recently exploited vulnerabilities affecting the organization's technology stack and provide awareness and recommendations to the appropriate internal teams.

- **IT and Infrastructure:** Leverage Threat Modelling to understand cyber threats and trends targeting the organization's sector and identify security enhancement implemented to reduce risk.

- **Application Support & Development:** Leverage Threat Modelling during the application development and Secure Software Development Lifecycle (SSDLC) process to provide a holistic approach to cyber threats and techniques used by threat actors to target organizations' applications and provide strategic recommendations during the development process.

- **Project Planning and Internal Initiatives:** Identify the context of key components within internal projects and initiatives and assess the potential threats that may be applicable.

Executive Buy-in

For a successful CTI team, it's essential to have executive buy-in for a successful cyber threat intelligence (CTI) program. This means there is support and interest from the Executive Management level of an organization to pursue CTI activities. Executive buy-in provides clear direction and the required funding for staffing resources, hardware and software, intelligence tools, community memberships, and data service and portal subscriptions. It also helps shape the CTI team and organizational structure, such as the roles and responsibilities of new positions. It supports intelligence requirements in their development and decisions regarding acquiring tools and other paid resources. Developing and implementing a successful CTI program is more manageable with executive buy-in.

The Executive Management's support will also help in the planning and preparation stages of the CTI program. It can shape the CTI team's organizational structure, such as determining the number of employees needed to support CTI operations and their roles and responsibilities. Additionally, it will support the development of intelligence requirements and assist in decisions regarding acquiring tools and other paid resources.

For example, a company's Executive Management team recognizes the importance of having a CTI program and allocates a budget for the necessary resources and staffing. This enables the CTI team to purchase intelligence tools and subscriptions, hire additional team members, and develop a clear plan for implementing the program. With this support, the program can get off the ground and have the necessary resources to be effective.

Support and involvement from executive management are vital aspects of a successful Cyber Threat Intelligence (CTI) initiative. This level of support enables the allocation of necessary resources and establishes a clear direction for the CTI team and program, ultimately contributing to its success.

Timely and Actionable Intelligence Products

Timely and actionable intelligence products are crucial for a successful Cyber Threat Intelligence (CTI) program. The output of the CTI team's activities should be in the form of products or services produced promptly to defend against emerging cyber threats effectively. These products should target the specific audience and threats impacting or potentially impacting the organization's technology stack and operations. Additionally, the products should be actionable and easily consumable by the receiving teams and security tools, ideally using automated means for rapid protection and defense. This allows for prompt defensive measures to be taken by the CTI team against emerging threats.

First and foremost, it is crucial to understand that the output of the activities of the Cyber Threat Intelligence Team will be some product or service. These products and services must be time to defend against emerging cyber threats effectively. One example is the WannaCry ransomware attacks that occurred several years ago. The sooner organizations knew about this threat, the better their chance of defending against it because the danger spread rapidly. Within a matter of hours, it affected hundreds of organizations worldwide.

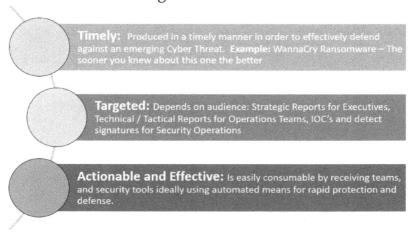

Timely: Produced in a timely manner in order to effectively defend against an emerging Cyber Threat. **Example:** WannaCry Ransomware – The sooner you knew about this one the better

Targeted: Depends on audience: Strategic Reports for Executives, Technical / Tactical Reports for Operations Teams, IOC's and detect signatures for Security Operations

Actionable and Effective: Is easily consumable by receiving teams, and security tools ideally using automated means for rapid protection and defense.

In addition to being timely, intelligence products must be targeted to the specific audience and threats impacting or impacting the organization. For example, a strategic report for executives would differ from a technical or tactical report for operations teams. Indicators of compromise (IOCs) and detection signatures for security operations must be tailored to the organization's specific technology stack and processes. If the products produced are not targeted, they will not be as effective in protecting the organization.

Lastly, intelligence products must be actionable and practical, so the receiving teams and security tools must easily consume them, ideally using automated means for rapid protection and defense. For example, indicators of compromise for a newly emerging ransomware variant can quickly and easily be integrated into a Security Information and Event Management (SIEM) system. In that case, it can result in prompt defensive measures taken by the Cyber Threat Intelligence Team.

Operational Security (OPSEC)

Operational security can be divided into two main aspects: protecting organizational assets during investigations and preventing threat actors from knowing that you are investigating them.

Protecting Organizational Assets:
When investigating malware samples, it is crucial to take precautions to avoid compromising your system or any other system on the corporate network. This is because malware can contain malicious code that could harm the systems and steal sensitive information. To mitigate this risk, one should use security tools such as malware sandboxes, and isolated environments designed explicitly for executing and analyzing malware samples. Additionally, it is crucial to consider the security implications of uploading files to free online tools, especially if they contain sensitive information. In such cases, it is advisable to use secure online tools that offer encryption and other security features to protect sensitive data.

Concealing Investigation from Threat Actors:
One of the biggest challenges in cybersecurity investigations is preventing potential threat actors from knowing they are being investigated. This is because such knowledge could prompt them to change tactics and make detecting their activities harder. To mitigate this risk, it is advisable to use VPNs, which encrypt internet traffic and conceal the public IP address. This makes it more difficult for threat actors to determine the location and organization of the person conducting the investigation. Another technique can be creating "sock puppet" accounts with fake identities. This can help conceal the digital footprint and prevent potential threat actors from tracing back to the organization.

Operational security plays a critical role in protecting organizational assets and ensuring the confidentiality of investigations. Using secure tools and techniques can reduce the risks associated with cybersecurity investigations and prevent potential threat actors from compromising sensitive information.

Metrics and Reporting

Metrics and reporting are essential to a CTI as they provide valuable insights and help demonstrate the program's value to the organization, leading to executive buy-in. It also helps track performance, operational efficiencies, and the value it brings by reducing risk to the overall organization. These metrics and other reporting also provide insight into the cyber threat landscape and help support strategic decisions and directions regarding security initiatives and controls.

It's essential to communicate the impact and value of the Cyber Threat Intelligence (CTI) team's work in reducing risk to the organization. This can be achieved using Key Risk Indicators (KRIs) and Key Performance Indicators (KPIs). KRIs are metrics that provide insight into potential risks to the organization and allow the CTI team to prioritize their efforts. For example, KRIs might include the number of successful phishing attempts, the frequency of successful ransomware attacks, or the number of vulnerabilities discovered and remediated.

By providing these meaningful KRIs to executives and stakeholders, the CTI team can effectively communicate the risk landscape and highlight areas where they have successfully reduced risk. Additionally, KPIs can be used to demonstrate the value of the CTI team's work in improving overall organizational performance.
For instance, KPIs might include:
- The time to detect and respond to threats.
- The percentage of threats that are successfully mitigated.
- The number of operational efficiencies achieved.

By presenting both KRIs and KPIs, the CTI team can effectively demonstrate the impact and value of their work in reducing risk and improving performance for the organization.

Reporting and metrics also provide insight into the cyber threat landscape and help support strategic decisions and directions regarding security. They emphasize initiatives and controls in place to reduce risk to the organization and can highlight improvements to operational efficiencies and detection capabilities. When producing these metrics and various reports, it's essential to be concise and provide the necessary information in an easily understandable format.

It's important to note that when producing these metrics and reports, it's crucial to be concise and ensure that the information is easily interpreted and highly visual. This will make it easier for stakeholders to understand and act upon the information provided.

Consumers and Stakeholders Feedback

As the Cyber Threat Intelligence (CTI) team develops and distributes its products and services, gathering user feedback is critical to enhance and improve the products and services continuously. User feedback should focus on new use cases, product suggestions, and any potential improvements that can be incorporated into the CTI team's offerings to better defend against cyber threats across the organization. By engaging with stakeholders and receiving their feedback, the CTI team can better understand the value of its products, identify areas for improvement, and drive operational efficiencies.

To maximize the effectiveness of the CTI program, it's essential to regularly meet with stakeholders to discuss the performance and impact of the products and services they receive. These discussions will help improve the overall CTI program, its offerings, and its operations. Feedback and collaboration with stakeholders is a crucial factors in ensuring that the CTI team continues to deliver high-quality and innovative products and services that support the organization's cyber defense efforts.

In conclusion, a successful CTI program requires a range of elements to be in place, including executive buy-in, actionable intelligence, robust operational security, and effective communication and collaboration within the organization. By focusing on these critical factors, organizations can improve their defenses against cyber threats and make informed decisions to enhance their security posture.

What you need to know when developing a CTI program.

Types of threat cyber threats that can affect your organization.

When developing a successful cyber threat intelligence program, it is important to know the different threats that can affect your organization. These can include technical threats, financial threats, and reputational threats.

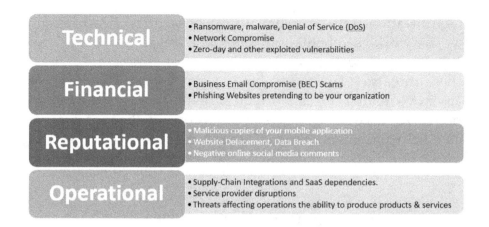

Technical threats such as ransomware, malware, and denial of service attacks can disrupt normal business operations and cause significant harm to an organization's IT infrastructure. Network compromises and 0-day vulnerabilities can allow cybercriminals to gain access to sensitive data, leading to data breaches and unauthorized access to critical systems.

Financial threats such as business email compromise scams and phishing websites can result in significant financial losses and damage an organization's reputation. Business email compromise scams target individuals within an organization's accounting department and can result in the transfer of large sums of money to unauthorized bank accounts. Phishing websites can lead to lost revenue and put clients' financial information at risk.

Reputational threats such as malicious mobile applications, website defacements, and data breaches can damage an organization's public image and reputation. Negative online social media comments and website defacements can also harm an organization's reputation and create a negative perception of the organization in the eyes of its clients and customers.

Organizations must implement robust security measures such as network segmentation, incident response plans, and employee education and awareness programs to mitigate these threats. It is also essential to continuously monitor and assess potential threats to an organization's systems and networks. A comprehensive cyber threat intelligence program can help organizations stay ahead of evolving threats and protect their assets, reputation, and bottom line.

What are your Security Capabilities

When creating a cyber threat intelligence (CTI) product, it is vital to understand the security capabilities of your organization and how the recipients of your CTI products and services can consume and use them. At the same time, understanding the data sources available to the CTI team can help to build better products.

Key questions that organizations should ask their IT network, network security teams, etc., include:
- What visibility do you have in the organization? This includes application logs, network traffic, user activity, and endpoint logs.
    - Can these be shared, and is there any helpful information that can be extracted for analysis and investigations to build detection signatures and identify cyber threats as they occur?

o What security tools and technologies does your organization have in place? This includes endpoint detection and response systems, intrusion detection and prevention systems, security information and event management systems, web application firewalls, and data loss prevention tools.

- What are the capabilities of these security tools? Can you add custom rules, search for data, see historical events easily, and integrate with external systems using common protocols like STIX or TAXII?
  o Are there ways to automate or sync information between systems for research and investigations?

It's also essential to understand the capabilities of the security tools and the way that they can be integrated with other systems:

- Can custom signatures be added?
- Can you search for data?
- Are there interactive capabilities?
- Can historical events be easily viewed?
- Is there an API or standard protocol for exchanging information?

Suppose your organization has endpoint detection tools in place. In that case, you should understand how to contribute detection rules, signatures, and other IOCs and extract reports. These could be helpful information for when intelligence requirements and associated products and services can be utilized.

Another critical aspect of building a CTI program is identifying subject matter experts within the organization. These experts can provide valuable information during investigations and assist in understanding how a threat exploits a specific aspect of the organization's infrastructure. For example, if you're investigating malware exploiting a vulnerability in Windows Server machines, a subject matter expert with extensive knowledge of the registry settings on Windows Server machines could be a valuable resource. These SMEs can become critical contacts for the CTI while performing intelligence investigations.

Establishing a comprehensive Cyber Threat Intelligence (CTI) program requires a thorough understanding of your organization's strengths and limitations. To effectively identify and respond to cyber threats, a combination of data sources, security tools, and subject matter experts should be leveraged. By utilizing all available resources, including relevant data, the full potential of security tools, and the expertise of internal personnel, organizations can create a robust CTI program that enables quicker and more efficient detection and response to cyber threats.

Who are your competitors and your supply chain

When addressing the cyber threat landscape, it is important to understand who your competitors and partners in the supply chain are, as their security incidents can also impact your organization. If a competitor or partner is compromised, it could be a precursor to other emerging threats or attacks within your industry. For example, if a threat actor is targeting trade secrets within an industry, and if you see other companies or competitors within your sector starting to get compromised, it may be a good idea to monitor what happened to them and how they got compromised and use that information to defend against similar attacks.

One of the most significant risks associated with a supply chain is the potential for cyber threats to target any of these entities. This scenario could happen in several ways, including phishing attacks, malware infections, or supply chain attacks. A supply chain attack is when an attacker targets a specific entity in the supply chain, such as a supplier, manufacturer, or service provider, to gain access to the larger organization.

An example of a supply chain attack that significantly impacted organizations was the SolarWinds attack in 2020. In this attack, a sophisticated threat actor was able to compromise the software updates of SolarWinds, a company that provides network management software to a wide range of organizations. This allowed the attacker to access the networks of SolarWinds' clients, including many government agencies and large corporations, upon pushing the updates to organizations running this software.

Another example is the NotPetya attack in 2017. This attack was launched by a group of cyber criminals targeting Ukraine, again through compromised software updates. The actors behind this malware propagated rapidly through the networks of organizations that had supply chain links to Ukraine. The malware was able to spread through these networks and cause significant damage, including data loss and system downtime.

When addressing the industry-wide threat landscape in your supply chain and competitors, it is essential to ask the following questions:
- What threats have your competitors and supply chain been experiencing?
- How have they been compromised, and if so, how?
- How would your organization be affected and given the same experience or situation?

- Could the same threats affect your organization?

These examples demonstrate the importance of organizations understanding and managing the risks associated with their supply chain. This includes conducting regular risk assessments, implementing security controls, and monitoring potential threats. It also includes developing incident response plans and working with trusted partners to share threat intelligence and coordinate responses. Organizations can better protect themselves and their supply chain from cyber threats by taking these steps.

Who are your customers

Monitoring online discussions about an organization is crucial as it provides insight into potential security risks and helps identify potential threats before they can cause harm. These discussions can take place on various platforms, including social media, forums, messaging apps, and even the dark web. Understanding the sentiment behind these conversations is essential, as evaluating whether they pose a security risk to the organization.

Once the source of the threat is identified, it's critical to assess the level of risk posed by the individual or group. This includes understanding the nature of the threat and its potential impact on the organization. For example, suppose a Facebook group discusses negative experiences with an organization's products or services. In that case, it could indicate a problem with the products or services, and further investigation may be necessary. On the other hand, if individuals discuss ways to exploit an organization's return policy, it could lead to financial loss and should be addressed promptly.

Building a CTI program is critical for organizations to stay ahead of security threats and maintain a secure environment. Monitoring online conversations and analyzing their sentiment is essential to this program. It helps organizations detect potential threats and take necessary measures to protect their assets and reputation. It's crucial to develop strategies to protect your organization. This may include working with law enforcement to go after your products' unauthorized sellers or developing a plan to address potential physical threats, such as protests or activism around your facility.

Who are your Adversaries?

As a cyber security professional, it is important to identify and understand the potential adversaries that may target your organization.

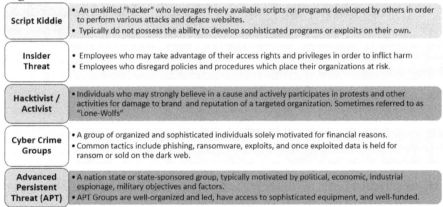

These adversaries can fall into several categories, including:

- **Script Kiddies:** unskilled hackers who use freely available scripts and programs to carry out low-level attacks, such as defacing websites.

- **Insider threats**: employees who may take advantage of their access rights and privileges to cause harm to the organization or disregard policies and procedures that put the organization at risk.

- **Hacktivists and Activists:** individuals or groups who gain unauthorized access to corporate data or networks to further social or political agendas. They may also actively participate in protests and other activities to damage the brand and reputation of a targeted organization.

- **Lone Wolves:** These individuals may have a personal vendetta against an organization and engage in cyber-attacks or other activities to cause harm.

- **Cybercrime Groups:** These are organized and sophisticated groups motivated by financial gain. They may use tactics such as phishing, ransomware exploits, and selling stolen data on the dark web.

- **Advanced Persistent Threats (APTs):** These are typically nation-states or state-sponsored groups motivated by political, economic, industrial, espionage, and military objectives. They are well-organized, well-funded, and have access to sophisticated equipment.

It is important to keep an eye out for these types of adversaries and to understand their tactics, techniques, and procedures to better protect your organization. Depending on the size of your organization and the products and services you offer, any combination of these adversaries may be of interest for further intelligence requirements. It's essential to be aware of the different types of adversaries and to develop a plan to protect your organization from their malicious intent.

The Cyber Threat Kill Chain

The Cyber Threat Kill Chain model provides organizations with a framework to understand and respond to cyber-attacks, as it allows them to identify the stage of the attack and take appropriate action to mitigate the risk. By understanding the steps involved in a cyber-attack, organizations can prioritize their efforts and allocate resources to defend against the most critical stages of the attack.

Phase	Description
Reconnaissance	• Identification of potential targets and their assets
Weaponization	• Creation of malicious payload or exploit.
Delivery	• Delivery of weaponized payload or exploit to victim phishing, drive-by-download, other vulnerabilities)
Exploitation	• Exploitation of vulnerabilities or other security weakness.
Installation	• Installation of malware on the victims' network
Command and Control	• Malware successfully deployed and beaconing awaiting further instructions
Action on Objectives	• Threat actor achieves their objectives

These phases include Reconnaissance, Weaponization, Delivery, Exploitation, Installation, Command and Control, and Action on Objectives.

- **Reconnaissance** involves identifying potential targets and assets, including enumeration of assets and potential targets.
- **Weaponization** is the creation of a malicious payload or exploit that allows the threat actor to gain access or deliver their intended actions.
- **Delivery** is the delivery of the weaponized payload to the target.
- **Exploitation** is the exploitation of security weaknesses to gain a foothold on the network.

- **Installation** of malware is the malware's persistence on the victim's network.
- **Command and control** is the ability for the threat actor to interact with the malware and issue commands.
- **Action on objectives** is the final goal of the threat actor.

Not every stage of the kill chain needs to be completed for a threat actor to achieve their goal.

As a cyber security professional, it is important to be aware of these phases and to have measures in place to detect and prevent them. This could include monitoring reconnaissance activities, implementing security controls to prevent Weaponization and exploitation, and having incident response plans for when malware is detected on the network. Additionally, it's essential to be aware of the different types of adversaries and their specific motivations, tactics, and level of sophistication. Understanding these concepts will help you better defend your organization against cyber threats.

The Traffic Light Protocol (TLP)

One important aspect of any threat intelligence program is the ability to share information effectively and securely. To accomplish this, many organizations use a framework known as the Traffic Light Protocol or TLP.

Color	When should it be used?
TLP:RED Not for disclosure, restricted to participants only.	Sources may use TLP:RED when information cannot be effectively acted upon by additional parties, and could lead to impacts on a party's privacy, reputation, or operations if misused.
TLP:AMBER Limited disclosure, restricted to participants' organizations.	Sources may use TLP:AMBER when information requires support to be effectively acted upon, yet carries risks to privacy, reputation, or operations if shared outside of the organizations involved.
TLP:GREEN Limited disclosure, restricted to the community.	Sources may use TLP:GREEN when information is useful for the awareness of all participating organizations as well as with peers within the broader community or sector.
TLP:WHITE Disclosure is not limited.	Sources may use TLP:WHITE when information carries minimal or no foreseeable risk of misuse, in accordance with applicable rules and procedures for public release.

Source: https://www.us-cert.gov/tlp

The TLP uses a color-coded system to indicate the level of sensitivity and distribution of information. The four colors used in the TLP are red, amber, green, and white.

- **Red:** This level is for highly sensitive information and restricted to only involved participants. This information should only be shared verbally or in person and must be confidential.

- **Amber:** This level is for information that requires support to be effectively acted upon, but carries privacy, reputational, and operational concerns if shared with outside parties. Information at this level can be shared within receiving organization but not outside of it.

- **Green:** This level is for information that is useful for all participating organizations and peers within a broader community or sector. The information can be shared within these peers and partners, but not publicly or via accessible channels.

- **White:** This level is for public information and can be distributed without restriction, subject to standard copyrights.

Using the TLP, organizations can effectively share information while ensuring that sensitive data is not accidentally shared with unauthorized parties. By following the TLP guidelines and communicating the level of sensitivity and distribution of information, organizations can better protect themselves and their partners from potential cyber threats.

Threatcon

ThreatCon is a critical component of an organization's overall cybersecurity strategy, as it helps to ensure that the appropriate measures are taken to protect against potential cyber threats. It is typically used by organizations in the public and private sectors and government agencies to respond to a perceived threat.

ThreatCon is a four-level system that assigns a threat level to an organization based on the perceived likelihood of a cyber-attack. The four levels are:

- **ThreatCon Normal:** This is the baseline threat level and indicates that no significant threats to the organization have been identified.

- **ThreatCon Elevated:** This level indicates that there is an increased likelihood of a cyber-attack, and organizations should take additional precautions to protect their systems and data.

- **ThreatCon High:** This level indicates a significant increase in the likelihood of a cyber-attack, and organizations should take immediate action to protect their systems and data.

- **ThreatCon Severe:** This is the highest threat level and indicates an imminent threat to the organization. Organizations should take immediate and extensive measures to protect their systems and data, including shutting down critical systems if necessary.

One of the key benefits of ThreatCon is that it enables organizations to respond to cyber threats promptly and effectively. Organizations can quickly assess the current threat level and take the necessary steps to protect their systems and data by having a standardized approach. This is especially important in fast-moving threat environments where threats can change rapidly, requiring organizations to respond quickly to protect their systems and data.

ThreatCon also enables organizations to be proactive in their approach to cybersecurity. By regularly reviewing the ThreatCon level and assessing the current threat environment, organizations can anticipate potential threats and take steps to mitigate the risks before an attack occurs. This proactive approach helps to reduce the impact of cyber-attacks and helps to ensure that the organization's systems and data remain secure.

The ThreatCon is an essential tool for organizations to manage the risks associated with cyber threats effectively. By providing a structured and consistent approach to assessing threat levels and determining the appropriate level of protection, organizations can respond to cyber threats promptly and effectively, helping to ensure the security of their systems and data.

The Intelligence Lifecycle

The intelligence lifecycle is a systematic process that is used to collect, analyze, and disseminate intelligence information. It consists of six stages: Planning and Direction, Collection, Processing, Analysis, Dissemination, and Feedback.

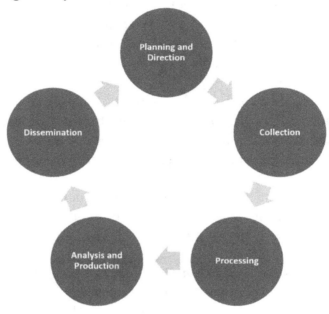

The cycle is comprised of several stages, including:

- **Planning and Direction:** In this stage, the intelligence requirements are defined and a plan is developed to collect the necessary information.

- **Collection:** This stage involves gathering information from various sources such as open-source intelligence (OSINT), human intelligence (HUMINT), signals intelligence (SIGINT), and geospatial intelligence (GEOINT).

- **Processing:** The collected information is processed and transformed into usable intelligence. This stage involves removing duplicates, classifying information, and verifying its accuracy.

- **Analysis:** The processed information is analyzed to determine its relevance and significance. Analysts use various techniques such as pattern analysis and link analysis to identify trends and relationships.

- **Dissemination:** The analyzed intelligence is disseminated to the relevant stakeholders. This stage involves sharing the intelligence through various channels such as reports, briefings, and secure communications.

Feedback is also a key component of the intelligence lifecycle as it involves evaluating the intelligence products, assessing the effectiveness of the intelligence-gathering effort, and making improvements for future cycles. The feedback allows professionals to assess the usefulness of the intelligence and adjust their approach for future collection and analysis.

An intelligence lifecycle is a critical tool in cyber security to ensure that organizations have access to accurate and timely intelligence to support their decision-making processes. By following this systematic approach, organizations can improve their ability to identify, respond to, and prevent cyber threats.

What resources do I need

A threat intelligence program is essential to an organization's overall security strategy. It helps organizations identify, assess, and respond to potential threats by providing them with actionable intelligence.

To develop and support a threat intelligence program, several resources are required:

- **Human Resource:** A dedicated team of security experts, including threat intelligence analysts, is required to develop, implement, and manage the threat intelligence program. This team should have the necessary skills, knowledge, and experience to collect, analyze, and disseminate threat intelligence.

- **Tools and Technologies:** Various tools and technologies are required to support a threat intelligence program, such as security information and event management (SIEM) systems, threat intelligence platforms, and data visualization tools. These technologies enable the collection, processing, analysis, and dissemination of threat intelligence.

- **Infrastructure:** As mentioned above the CTI team will require tools and technologies to support their operations and investigations. This includes computing and storage for applications, tools, and scripts that the CTI team will use.

- **Data:** Threat intelligence programs require a wide range of data sources, including internal and external data. External data sources include open-source intelligence, commercial intelligence feeds, and third-party threat intelligence services. Internal data sources include logs, network traffic, and security alerts generated by security tools.

- **Procedures and Processes:** The development of standard operating procedures (SOPs) and processes are essential to a successful threat intelligence program. These procedures and processes should outline the steps required to collect, analyze, disseminate, and act on threat intelligence.

- **Budget:** A budget is required to support the development and implementation of a threat intelligence program. This budget should cover the costs of personnel, technologies, data, and training.

- **Training:** A threat intelligence program requires regular training for the team members to keep them updated with the latest threat intelligence techniques, technologies, and trends.

It's important to understand that with these resources, an organization may be able to effectively identify, assess, and respond to potential cyber threats. For example, with access to advanced technologies and data sources, an organization may be able to accurately gather and analyze intelligence, making it easier to make informed decisions about threat mitigation and response. Similarly, with a well-trained and knowledgeable threat intelligence team, an organization may have the necessary expertise to make sense of the data and apply it to the threat landscape.

It's also crucial to continuously review and update the threat intelligence program to ensure that it remains aligned with the organization's objectives and the evolving threat landscape. The cyber threat landscape is constantly changing, and new threats and attack methods are continually being developed. As such, organizations must continuously assess and update their threat intelligence programs to ensure they are equipped to handle new and emerging threats.

Human Resources

As a cyber security professional, it is important to understand the human resources requirements for a cyber threat intelligence (CTI) team. The scope of the intelligence requirements and budget will determine the necessary roles and resources. These roles can be filled internally through full-time employees (FTEs), internal contractors, or leveraging third-party teams such as managed security service providers or other threat intelligence vendors.

When starting, the resources required for CTI operations may only require a portion of a full-time employee. As the program grows, additional resources may be required. For a successful CTI team, members must have various experiences and expertise, including knowledge in areas such as information security, data analysis, and intelligence gathering. This will ensure that the team can effectively collect, analyze, and disseminate threat intelligence to support the organization's security efforts.

* Sample Cyber-Treat Intelligence Team Structure

For a successful CTI team, it is best to have members with various experiences and expertise. This includes individuals with technical expertise in network security, malware analysis, and incident response, as well as individuals with expertise in intelligence analysis, research, and data analysis. Having diverse skills and experiences in the CTI team will allow them to be more effective in identifying, assessing, and responding to potential threats.

Additionally, it's essential to have a team leader who can coordinate the team's efforts, develop and implement the CTI strategy, and ensure that the intelligence produced is actionable and in line with the organization's objectives. The team lead should have a strong understanding of the organization's business, the threat landscape, and the intelligence requirements.

Tools and Technologies

A cyber threat intelligence program requires various technologies to effectively collect, analyze, and disseminate threat intelligence. Some key technologies include:

- **Security Information and Event Management (SIEM):** systems collect and aggregate log data from various sources, such as network devices, servers, and applications, to provide a centralized view of security events. SIEMs can be used to identify potential threats and vulnerabilities and to track the activity of known threat actors.

- **Threat intelligence platforms (TIPs):** platforms provide the ability to collect, store, and analyze intelligence data from multiple sources, including OSINT, commercial and community feeds. TIPs can also be used to automate the correlation of different data sources and to identify new threats and vulnerabilities.

- **Data visualization tools:** tools are used to present, correlate, and interpret threat intelligence data in a clear and easy-to-understand manner, making it easier for analysts to identify patterns and trends.

- **Malware analysis tools:** tools used to analyze and reverse-engineer malware, providing valuable insights into the malware's behavior, capabilities, and command and control infrastructure.

- **Network traffic analysis tools:** used to monitor and analyze network traffic, identifying potential malicious activity and tracking the activity of known threat actors.

- **Automation tools:** automation tools can be used to automate various tasks such as data collection, analysis, and correlation that are required for a cyber threat intelligence program.

It's essential to assess your specific needs and requirements to ensure that you choose tools that will provide actionable intelligence that aligns with your goals. When choosing these tools, it's essential to weigh their benefits against their cost to ensure that their value justifies their expenses.

It's worth noting that tools are only one piece of the puzzle for producing cyber threat intelligence products and services. They are simply a tool that provides raw data and output, which must then be reviewed and analyzed by an intelligence analyst to produce intelligence products that can be used to make informed decisions.

The real value of cyber threat intelligence lies not in the tools themselves but in the interpretation, analysis, and ability to use the output to inform decision-making processes. In other words, tools are the means to an end, and the intelligence analyst's expertise and analysis provide the actual value in producing effective and impactful intelligence products and services.

Infrastructure

When it comes to cyber threat intelligence, having the proper infrastructure in place is crucial. This includes the type of computer or server you use and the environment in which the tools are run. Most intelligence tools are Linux based, so it's best to run them on a Linux desktop or server. A typical configuration for running these tools would be a Linux server with 20 gigs of hard drive space and four gigs of RAM. More sophisticated Intelligence Tools and database systems are also available that may require some robust systems to operate the tools efficiently. It is important to note that when identifying valuable tools for your CTI program, you evaluate their dependencies to ensure that you can support the operations of those tools.

Some key components of this infrastructure include:

- **Data storage:** A robust data storage solution is required to store the large amounts of data generated by a threat intelligence program. This data must be securely stored, easily accessible, and backed up to ensure continuity of operations.

- **Network infrastructure:** A secure and reliable network infrastructure is necessary to support the collection, analysis, and dissemination of threat intelligence. This may include firewalls, intrusion detection and prevention systems, and secure communication protocols.

- **Computing resources:** A cyber threat intelligence program requires a significant amount of computing resources, including servers, storage, and processing power, to support the collection, analysis, and dissemination of threat intelligence.

- **Automation capabilities:** Automation capabilities, such as scripting and programming, are necessary to support the collection, analysis, and dissemination of threat intelligence. This can include data collection, correlation, analysis, and the automation of reporting and alerting.

- **Access controls:** Access controls are necessary to ensure that only authorized personnel can access sensitive threat intelligence data. This may include user authentication, role-based access, and multi-factor authentication.

Virtual environments, such as virtualized servers or desktops within your environment, can also work well. This could include virtualization solutions like VMware, Virtual Box, or cloud infrastructures like AWS, Google Compute, or Azure. It's recommended to run tools, scripts, and intelligence programs on separate systems and a segregated network. This prevents cross-contamination between activities and actions done by the cyber threat intelligence team and the rest of corporate operations and reduces the risk of a security incident affecting other devices on the corporate network.

Having the proper infrastructure is crucial for effective cyber threat intelligence. Choosing the right operating system, virtual environment, and network segregation is important to ensure that your intelligence tools, scripts, and programs are running securely and efficiently.

Data

Having a diverse range of data and data sources is essential for a CTI team to identify and assess potential cyber threats effectively. Using multiple sources, they can ensure they have complete information, validate data accuracy, and gain a more comprehensive view. This leads to informed decisions on threat prioritization and effective responses.

Some key data sources include:

- **Open-source intelligence data (OSINT):** such as information from social media, news articles, and forums, is free and can be a great starting point for most intelligence requirements. However, it may require additional tools and effort to vet, clean up, and enrich the information to make it useful.

- **Commercial platforms:** such as Recorded Future or Intel 471, typically already have vetted, structured, and enriched data, making it more ready to use for intelligence requirements. These types of platforms can also streamline and automate intelligence requirements activities.

- **Commercial intelligence feeds:** These are paid services that provide access to a wide range of data such as cybercrime data, threat actor information, and malware intelligence. They can be a valuable resource for identifying specific threats and vulnerabilities.

- **Internally generated logs and data:** such as application and system logs, can also be a valuable source of information for a cyber threat intelligence team. This data can provide insights into the organization's specific threat landscape and can be used to identify and respond to potential threats.

- **Dark web and underground data:** Some threat intelligence teams also monitor the dark web and underground forums for information on potential threats.

- **External partners:** Sharing threat intelligence with external partners such as other companies, government agencies or industry groups can provide a valuable perspective on potential threats and vulnerabilities.

When starting, open-source data may be sufficient for most intelligence requirements. However, as a CTI program matures, commercial data and platforms may become valuable resources to streamline and automate intelligence gathering.

A cyber threat intelligence team requires diverse data sources to identify, assess, and respond to potential threats. The data sources range from publicly available open-source intelligence to paid commercial feeds and internally generated data. They also require monitoring underground and dark web sources and sharing information with external partners to get a complete perspective on the threat landscape.

Processes, Procedures and Playbooks

Standard Operating Procedures (SOPs), Playbooks, and Runbooks are essential for a successful Threat Intelligence program as they provide clear and concise guidance for collecting, analyzing, disseminating, and responding to cyber threats. These documents serve as structured, step-by-step guides and a reference for CTI teams, reducing the chances of human error and ensuring consistency in handling threat intelligence. The development and maintenance of these documents are crucial for ensuring the effectiveness of a Threat Intelligence program.

Benefits of documented CTI processes, procedures include:

- **Threat intelligence collection:** help organizations to identify the most relevant sources of threat intelligence and establish criteria for collecting and processing this information. This can help ensure that the CTI team is collecting high-quality, relevant data that can effectively respond to threats.

- **Threat analysis:** outline the steps required for analyzing threat intelligence, including various tools and techniques for assessing the severity, likelihood, and impact of potential threats. This can help to ensure that the CTI team has a consistent and effective approach to threat analysis.

- **Threat response:** provide clear guidance on responding to threats, including the steps required to take action and minimize the impact of a potential attack. This can help to ensure that the organization is prepared and equipped to respond quickly and effectively to cyber threats.

- **Collaboration and communication:** promote effective communication and collaboration between the CTI team, other security teams, and stakeholders. This can help to ensure that everyone is working towards the same goal and that the CTI team can effectively share its findings and recommendations with relevant stakeholders.

- **Continual improvement:** should be regularly reviewed and updated to ensure that they remain relevant and up to date. This can help to ensure that the organization's security posture is continually improving and that the CTI team can respond effectively to changing threat landscapes.

These documents serve as the foundation for effective threat intelligence and must reflect any changes or updates to the program, processes, or technologies used. By maintaining these documents regularly, organizations can ensure that their CTI program stays current and relevant, which is critical in the fast-paced and ever-evolving threat landscape. Keeping these documents up to date also helps enhance an organization's security posture by providing clear and consistent guidance to the CTI team on how to identify, assess, and respond to cyber threats. This not only enables organizations to be better prepared in the face of cyber-attacks but also makes them more resilient and less vulnerable to future threats.

Budget

One of the key components of a CTI budget is staffing. Organizations need to invest in hiring and training dedicated CTI analysts to form a robust CTI team. This team should have the expertise and knowledge to collect, analyze, and disseminate threat intelligence effectively. Investing in staffing should also provide opportunities for continuous professional development to keep the team updated with the latest threat intelligence practices and technologies.

Another critical aspect of the CTI budget is the investment in technology and tools. Organizations must have access to relevant intelligence feeds, threat intelligence platforms, and analytics tools to support their CTI efforts. Having the necessary technology in place enables the CTI team to gather high-quality, relevant threat data and provide a comprehensive view of the threat landscape. Organizations may sometimes need to invest in external support, such as consulting or threat intelligence services, to supplement their internal CTI capabilities. This can provide the CTI team with additional expertise and resources and help ensure that the organization's overall security posture continues to improve.

A robust CTI budget can significantly enhance an organization's threat visibility, improve threat analysis capabilities, reduce response times, improve collaboration and communication, and maintain a strong security posture. By investing in a comprehensive CTI budget, organizations can minimize the impact of potential attacks and protect their valuable assets.

Training

Investing in Cyber Threat Intelligence (CTI) training and professional development is key in ensuring that organizations can effectively respond to cyber threats. This is particularly important in today's rapidly evolving threat landscape, where new and sophisticated threats are constantly emerging. By investing in CTI personnel, organizations can ensure that they have the necessary skills and knowledge to identify, assess, and respond to cyber threats promptly and effectively.

The key components of CTI training and professional development should include understanding the fundamentals of CTI, advanced CTI techniques, cybersecurity concepts, and technical training in relevant tools and technologies. The fundamentals of CTI include the collection and analysis of threat intelligence, the dissemination of threat intelligence, and the development of response plans. Personnel should have a solid understanding of these concepts to contribute to the organization's CTI program effectively.

Advanced CTI techniques include malware analysis, threat intelligence, and incident response. Personnel should be well-versed in these techniques to analyze and respond to threats promptly and effectively. Cybersecurity concepts and technologies should also be covered in CTI training, as this will give personnel a better understanding of the latest threats and trends in the cybersecurity landscape. Technical training in the tools and technologies used to support CTI is also critical. This includes intelligence feeds, threat intelligence platforms, and analytics tools. Personnel should have the necessary skills and knowledge to use these tools to support their CTI activities effectively.

By investing in CTI personnel, organizations can see numerous benefits, including improved threat intelligence, faster response times, better collaboration and communication, continual improvement, and a competitive advantage in the face of cyber threats. Improved threat intelligence means organizations can have more accurate, relevant, and actionable information, improving their security posture. Faster response times allow organizations to minimize the impact of potential attacks, reducing the potential for harm. Effective collaboration and communication between the CTI team, other security teams, and stakeholders ensures that everyone is working towards the same goal. By investing in training and professional development, organizations can ensure that their CTI personnel continually improve their skills and knowledge, leading to a continually improving security posture. Finally, having well-trained and knowledgeable CTI personnel gives organizations a competitive advantage in the face of cyber threats, helping to ensure they remain one step ahead of potential attackers.

Investing in CTI training and professional development is essential for organizations to be better prepared and more resilient to cyber threats. By having the necessary skills and knowledge, organizations can minimize the impact of potential attacks and maintain a strong security posture. By investing in their personnel, organizations can ensure they are well-equipped to respond to the latest threats and trends in the rapidly evolving threat landscape.

Summary

This chapter introduces readers to the fundamental concepts and terminology related to cyber-threat intelligence, including its advantages and capabilities. They were also introduced to various types of adversaries and the factors that contributed to the success of a CTI program, including stakeholder and executive support. The cyber threat kill-chain, the threat con, and the traffic light protocol was explored as the intelligence lifecycle, which encompasses collecting, analyzing, and distributing intelligence.

The next chapter focuses on the discovery phase of building a CTI program which is a crucial step in identifying and cataloging sensitive assets within an organization vulnerable to cyber threats. A comprehensive inventory list is essential to the success of a CTI program as it provides a foundation for developing intelligence and collection requirements and a reference point for assessing the potential impact of emerging cyber threats on the organization. The discovery chapter will be the basis for building a CTI program, and each chapter will build upon activities performed in previous chapters. It is critical to take the time to identify and document all relevant assets accurately.

Chapter #2 – Discovery

Introduction

The Discovery of assets for a Cyber Threat Intelligence (CTI) program is essential in identifying and understanding potential cyber threats that could impact an organization. This process is crucial in identifying and understanding potential cyber threats that could impact an organization. The objective is to discover physical and digital assets within the organization and document the associated supply chain, dependencies, vendors, and service providers.

To achieve this, the CTI team should involve stakeholders and conduct interviews to identify critical systems, technologies, data, brands, products, and organizational crown jewels. This will help understand the business context of assets and resources that support vital functions and identify stakeholders and internal teams that can benefit from CTI products and services. Moreover, discovering data sources within the organization will aid in cyber threat detection and enrichment capabilities.

Discovery	• Document physical and digital assets used within the organization. • Document Supply Chain, vendors and service providers. • Identify keywords, terms & phrases for monitoring • Identify internal data logs and sources
Risk assessment and threat modelling	• Determine the risks and threats associated with corporate assets. • Model high-level threat scenarios that can impact your organization. • Categorize threat scenarios to support the development of intelligence requirements and/or use cases.

The information gathered during the asset discovery process will be used for Threat Modeling in the next phase. This will determine the various corporate assets' associated threats and model high-level threat scenarios that could impact the organization. The information will also support the development of intelligence requirements and use cases, categorized based on the threat scenarios.

The asset discovery process can be done through a simple Excel or Word document or commercial asset discovery and tracking tools. The information collected should include the item, technical details, and a description. Examples of the information that should be collected are primary corporate domains, DNS servers, primary server operating systems, desktop and employee laptops, IP spaces, network services, software, and applications, etc. It's important to note that each line of business may have its unique corporate assets, including digital assets such as websites, proprietary applications, processes or algorithms, physical assets, brands and products, technical assets, and social media accounts.

During the process, valuable data, such as log files, may be uncovered, which can be used as input for intelligence requirements. It's essential to note these assets on the asset inventory documents to flag them as potential data sources if required. Additionally, the process aims to establish contacts with subject matter experts from various lines of business to support the discovery initiatives, identify internal data sources that can be leveraged for the detection and enrichment of threat intelligence services, and identify areas where the CTI team can collaborate and complement other security teams.

Chapter Objectives

The discovery phase in a cyber security program is crucial for identifying and documenting an organization's sensitive assets, information, intellectual property, and technologies. By understanding the business context of these assets, organizations can prioritize their security efforts and align them with their internal risk management strategies and business requirements. This information is then used to develop a comprehensive security plan and prioritize allocating resources to protect critical assets. The discovery phase is crucial in ensuring the adequate protection of sensitive assets and information.

Upon completion of this chapter, participants will be able to:
- Identify critical assets, technologies, and data that support the organization's ability to produce its products or services.
- Understand the business context of assets and resources that support critical functions.
- Prioritize efforts consistent with internal risk management strategies and business requirements.
- Identify stakeholders and internal teams that can benefit from CTI products and services.
- Discover data sources within the organization that can assist in cyber threat detection and data enrichment capabilities.

The discovery phase is critical in ensuring that organizations are equipped with the information they need to effectively protect their sensitive assets, information, intellectual property, and technologies. By understanding the business context of these assets, organizations can align their security efforts with their risk management strategies and business requirements, ensuring that they are better prepared to respond to potential security threats.

Discovery activities

The first step in intelligence discovery is to list all the assets and technologies used within your organization. These assets play a critical role in the functioning of your organization and, if unavailable, could pose service or operational issues. To keep track of these assets, you can use a simple Excel or Word document if the data can be structured for filtering purposes. You can also use commercial asset discovery and tracking tools available on the market.

For example, the primary corporate domains, DNS servers, primary server operating systems, primary desktops, and laptops. Also, IP address spaces, both internal subnets and public subnets. This is an example, but we need to collect and categorize this data.

This information will be helpful later as we develop intelligence requirements. The best way to discover critical assets within an organization is to meet with stakeholders to identify their assets, crown jewels, essential systems and technology, necessary data, key brands, products, and so on.

Another objective of the discovery activities is to establish subject matter experts for various lines of business who can support the discovery initiatives. We also need to identify stakeholders with internal data sources that could be leveraged for detection capabilities and enrichment for threat intelligence services.

We also want to identify where threat intelligence can complement other security teams.

As you go through your discovery activities, you will gain a bigger picture of how the organization works and where else you can identify other subject matter experts who can assist. You'll also find out where other data teams and security teams should be included to provide their input to the threat intelligence team and, potentially, an output from the threat intelligence team to produce a product or service that these other teams and subject matter experts can consume.

Each line of business may have its unique corporate assets, including digital assets such as websites, proprietary applications, processes, or algorithms. Physical assets could include office locations, satellite locations, data centers, and other physical assets, such as storefronts for retail locations or manufacturing locations for industrial manufacturers. Brands and products the business has or operates, technical assets including servers, network segments, hardware, software, and, Social media accounts, which could include corporate and high-profile employee accounts. It's essential to keep an inventory of these accounts and monitor them for potential spoofed accounts that could provide misleading or derogatory information about your organization.

In addition, we need to identify dependencies such as service providers like internet service providers, telecommunications providers, domain hosting providers, web hosting providers, and so on. If you're in a manufacturing or retail environment, you'll also need to identify dependencies in your supply chain and key software that you're running.

These dependencies are critical to the operations and security of your organization. These typically include intellectual property, patents, proprietary, and supply chain industry, and you'll want to consider the dependencies on vendors, suppliers, and partners.

The discovery activities are crucial in building a comprehensive Cyber Threat Intelligence program. They provide a foundation for understanding the organization's assets and technologies and identifying key stakeholders and potential data sources for threat intelligence.

It also helps to identify areas where threat intelligence can complement other security teams and initiatives.

Data Collection

Company Details

The first step in creating an effective CTI program is to gather comprehensive information about the organization, including its business context and operating model. This information provides valuable insights into the organization's structure, operations, and the type of assets it holds, allowing the CTI team to develop a comprehensive list of keywords for threat detection.

One of the key benefits of having a comprehensive understanding of the organization is that it enables the CTI team to detect targeted and potential threats. By knowing the company's subsidiaries, competitors, brands, products, and dependencies, the team can develop a targeted list of keywords and monitor for any suspicious activity. This information can also help the team identify potential vulnerabilities and prioritize their response based on the organization's assets and operations.

Description	Company_Details
IronCo Steel and Manufacturing	Company Name
982 Main Street Suite 204, Toronto, Ontario	Company Address
1087 Industrial Way, Toronto, Ontario	Company Address
1 (416) 543-8722	Company Phone number
1 (416) 903-2443	Company Phone number
Manufacturing	Primary Industry / Sector
Metals	Other Related Industry Sectors
IronCo Nails and Rebar	Subsidiaries
Mitchell Steel	Competitors
Novant Steel	Competitors
Raw Steel Products Ltd.	Competitors
TICK.to	Stock Market Ticker

One of the key benefits of having a comprehensive understanding of the organization is that it enables the CTI team to detect targeted and potential threats. By knowing the company's subsidiaries, competitors, brands, products, and dependencies, the team can develop a targeted list of keywords and monitor for any suspicious activity. This information can also help the team identify potential vulnerabilities and prioritize their response based on the organization's assets and operations.

In some cases, the information needed to create a comprehensive CTI program may be available through something other than internal logs or visibility sources. The team may rely on external sources such as open-source intelligence-gathering techniques, web scraping, social media monitoring, and data breaches. It's important to remember that data collected from external sources should be thoroughly verified and validated before being used in any analysis. This ensures that the information used for CTI operations is reliable and trustworthy, providing a solid foundation for the overall CTI program.

In conclusion, gathering information about an organization is crucial in creating an effective CTI program. By comprehensively understanding the organization's business context and operating model, the CTI team can develop a targeted list of keywords for threat detection, prioritize responses based on assets and operations, and mitigate cyber threats proactively.

Critical components of an organization

Identifying critical assets, processes, and technologies is crucial in the Cyber Threat Intelligence (CTI) process. This helps the CTI team understand the underlying motivations of threat actors, including their objectives for accessing sensitive information and disrupting operations. A comprehensive understanding of these critical components is essential in providing a comprehensive overview of the organization's business context and can serve as a valuable reference for CTI operations.

Description:	Critical_Type	Location
Cold Rolling Line	Technology	1087 Industrial Way, Toronto, Ontario
Steel Pickling Line	Technology	1087 Industrial Way, Toronto, Ontario
Raw Materials	Assets	1087 Industrial Way, Toronto, Ontario
Metal Finishing	Processes	1087 Industrial Way, Toronto, Ontario
Accounting	Processes	982 Main Street Suite 204, Toronto, Ontario
Quality Assurance	Processes	1087 Industrial Way, Toronto, Ontario
Logistics	Processes	1087 Industrial Way, Toronto, Ontario

In identifying these critical assets, processes, and technologies, it is also imperative to determine their physical locations and the availability of any relevant data sources that can be used for threat-hunting and data enrichment activities. Logs generated by these assets, processes, and technologies can provide valuable insights into the operations of the organization and can serve as useful data sources for investigative and enrichment activities.

For example, logs generated by different systems and technologies that monitor and automate organizational processes, such as manufacturing techniques, can provide valuable information for threat-hunting and data enrichment activities. Utilizing these logs as data sources can help enhance the visibility of the organization's operations and offer actionable insights to mitigate cyber threats.

Identifying critical assets, processes, and technologies is crucial in building an effective Cyber Threat Intelligence program. It allows the CTI team to understand the motivations of threat actors and disrupt their operations while also providing valuable data sources for threat-hunting and data enrichment activities.

Technical dependencies of an organization

The next step in the Cyber Threat Intelligence (CTI) process is to delve deeper into the technical details of the organization, including the infrastructure, network security tools, and applications that the company regularly uses. This includes examining the company's infrastructure, network security tools, and applications.

A critical starting point is determining if the organization has an existing hardware or software inventory application. This can serve as a valuable resource and speed up data collection.

Item	Technical_Detail	Description
ironco.local	Primary Corporate Domain	internal corporate domain
192.168.x.x	Private Address Space used	Internal network range
Windows 11 Desktop	Primary Desktop OS	Employee workstations
Windows Server 2019	Primary Server OS	Corporate servers and systems
RedHat Linux v8.6	Secondary DataBase Server OS	Primarily DataBase Servers
MsSQL 2019	Databases	used for E
MySQL v18.7	Databases	used for ERM software
Metlurg Analysis	Software and Application	Metal QA Analysis Software
Chrome v 91.14.31.5	Software and Application	Primary Web Broswer
Adobe Acrobat v19.2	Software and Application	Primary PDF Reader
SolarWinds v14.2	Security Applications, Appliances, and Tools	Network Management
Microsoft Defender	Security Applications, Appliances, and Tools	End-Point Anti-Virus
YubiKeys	Security Applications, Appliances, and Tools	MFA
Juniper Firewall jOS 18.7	Perimeter Protection Devices	Firewall
144.82.34.0/24	IP Address ranges (in CIDR format)	Public Facing IP Addresses

When collecting technical information, it's imperative to ensure that all relevant details, such as software versions, are captured to provide a comprehensive view of the organization's technological assets. This information can be used to quickly identify if the organization is using software that is vulnerable to known exploits. For example, the CTI team can gather data on the organization's domain, internal subnets, desktop and server operating systems, and a list of applications, including, but not limited to, Microsoft SQL, Windows Server 2019, Microsoft Defender, cloud resources, network applications, and services, among others. This information provides a high-level view of the organization's technical landscape and can be used to understand the purpose and potential use of these assets as sources of information.

Identifying critical assets, processes, and technologies is essential for building an effective CTI program. By understanding the underlying motivations of threat actors, the CTI team can effectively hunt for threats and enhance data sources for threat intelligence. Furthermore, identifying logs and other outputs generated by these assets and the organization's infrastructure, network security tools, and applications can provide valuable context for monitoring and investigation activities.

Domains used by an Organization

In today's increasingly digital world, having a robust online presence through a well-maintained website domain is essential for organizations to reach and interact effectively with their customers and clients. The website domain serves as a platform for communication, marketing, and showcasing the organization's products and services to the public. However, the growing importance of website domains has also made them an attractive target for cybercriminals and threat actors. These malicious individuals and organizations often exploit vulnerabilities in websites to steal sensitive information, spread malware, and disrupt business operations.

Registered Domain Names	Domain Registrars	IP Address
www.IronCo.ca	GoDaddy	144.82.34.88
www.IronCo.com	HostPapa	144.82.34.87
NewMetalToday.com	Digital Ocean	144.82.34.72

Organizations need to be proactive in managing and protecting their website domains. A critical first step is to keep a comprehensive record of all domains and websites used by the organization. This will allow the organization to quickly identify and assess potential threats and vulnerabilities and take prompt action to mitigate them. For example, by regularly monitoring their domains for signs of suspicious activity, organizations can quickly detect and respond to attempts to exploit vulnerabilities.

Website domain security is a critical aspect of overall cyber security that organizations cannot afford to ignore. By maintaining a comprehensive record of their domains, implementing strong security measures, and regularly monitoring for threats, organizations can ensure the security of their online presence and protect their valuable assets from cyber threats.

Social Media accounts of the organization

Social media has become an integral part of our lives, and organizations use it to connect with their customers and promote their products and services. However, the widespread use of social media has also opened new avenues for malicious actors to target organizations and their customers.

One of the primary ways malicious actors can harm organizations and their customers is by creating fake or misleading social media accounts that impersonate legitimate ones. These fake accounts can be used to spread false information, deliver malware, or steal credentials through phishing attacks. As a result, organizations must be vigilant in monitoring both legitimate and illegitimate social media accounts associated with their brand.

Platform:	Account Name(s) / Identifiers:	Account URL	Who Internally Manages
Twitter	@IronCo	https://twitter/@IronCo	Social Media Team
Instagram	@IronCo	https://instagram.com/@IronCo	Social Media Team
Facebook	@IronCo	https://Facebook.com/IronCo	Social Media Team
Facebook	@IronCo - Future of Metal Group	/Facebook.com/groups/IronCo-Future_of	Product Team
Youtube	@IronCo	https://youtube.com/@ironco	Social Media Team
LinkedIn	IronCo	https://LinkedIn.com/IronCo	Social Media Team
LinkedIn	Co - Innovations in Metal Production Gr	https://LinkedIn.com/groups/IronCo-Inn	Product Team

Keeping a comprehensive list of all the social media accounts associated with the organization is the first step in proactively monitoring these accounts. This list should include all legitimate accounts and any known illegitimate ones. Organizations can use various tools, such as social media monitoring platforms, to keep track of their accounts and their activity on them.

Regular monitoring of the accounts will help organizations identify and respond to any malicious activities or suspicious behavior, such as the spread of false information or the delivery of malware. By detecting such activities early, organizations can minimize damage to their reputation and protect their customers from potential harm. As a result, organizations must take proactive steps to monitor both legitimate and illegitimate social media accounts associated with their brand and take action to protect their customers and reputation.

Key people

Cyber Threat Intelligence (CTI) is a crucial component of a comprehensive cybersecurity program. A critical aspect of building a successful CTI program is understanding the employee hierarchy within an organization. Identifying the key decision-makers and executives within the organization is imperative, as cyber criminals often target them.

One such threat to these high-level individuals is social media spoofing. Threat actors may create fake social media accounts impersonating these executives to spread false information, promote malicious applications, or gain access to sensitive information. For example, a threat actor may target an IT administrator through social media, posing as a trusted source to obtain access to service provider accounts such as Host Papa or GoDaddy.

Name	People_Type	Role	Description
Sharon Speals	Executive and Board	CEO	Chief Executive Officer
Glen Gordon	Executive and Board	CFO	Chief Financial Officer
Tina McAllister	Employees	Lead Accountant	Prepare Accounting Documents for Approval
Allen Wong	Employees	Senior Manager - Accounting	Signs off on Accounting Approvals
Gloria Shuster	Employees	Sr Financial Analyst	Prepares Accounting Approvals for Review
Accounting Team	Internal Teams	N/A	All team including jr. team members
Internal Products Team	Internal Teams	N/A	Develops new products for the company and handles confident Intellictural Proper
Greg Clark	Employees	Sr. IT Analyst	Domain Administrator
Jennifer Clarister	Employees	Sr. IT Analyst	Cloud Administrator

Another critical area of concern for CTI teams is business email compromise scams. This threat involves fake invoice scams or funds transfer to false accounts. Threat actors, who have already gained access to a compromised email account, impersonate legitimate vendors or suppliers to trick employees into making payments to the wrong bank accounts. For example, the threat actor may reply to an accounts payable person pretending to be from XYZ Company and request that payment credentials be changed to a different bank account.

To help identify key people and potential risks within an organization, CTI teams can use a risk matrix. This matrix can help to determine the sensitivity of sensitive employees and prioritize the resources and attention given to each area. By taking a proactive and comprehensive approach to CTI, organizations can better defend against cyber threats and protect their critical assets.

This should be a manageable list. To help identify key people and potential risks within an organization, CTI teams may use a risk matrix like the one shown below to determine the sensitivity of sensitive employees.

Level	Security	Accounting	IT	Other Corporate Staff
Junior	Low	Low	Low	Low
Senior	Medium	Medium	Medium	Low
Management	High	High	Medium	Medium
Director	High	High	High	Medium
Executive Leadership	High	High	High	High

This sample matrix can be used to understand who should be included on the CTI team's list of high-risk individuals. For example, junior members of teams may need access to sensitive information. They would be considered low risk, while senior individuals in security or accounting positions could be considered medium risk. Management, directors, and executives would be regarded as high-risk individuals. Targeting these people or fake accounts from these people could pose a direct risk internally or to clients and consumers.

Understanding the employee pyramid structure and identifying key people is crucial for a successful CTI program. By monitoring spoofed social media accounts and keeping an eye out for business email compromise scams, CTI teams can help protect the organization from a wide range of cyber threats.

Service Providers

This section will discuss the importance of a comprehensive understanding of the service providers utilized by your organization and the impact they can have on your systems and data security and privacy. This includes well-known providers such as Bell and Rogers and smaller providers that may be less frequent in the news.

It is essential to regularly monitor these providers for any security vulnerabilities or breaches that may affect the specific services and applications used by the organization. For example, cloud providers like Amazon Web Services and Microsoft Azure, email providers like Google G Suite and Microsoft Office 365, and software-as-a-service providers like Salesforce and Zendesk are commonly used by organizations and often store sensitive data. Therefore, staying up to date on any security incidents that may impact these services is crucial.

Name:	Service Provided:	Details:
Bell Canada	Internet	Internet Connection for the main office
Rogers	Internet	Internet Connection for the factory
Telus	Phone Service	Factory and Office Phone lines
Microsoft Azure	Office365	Microsoft Office Licensing
HydroOne	Electricity	Power for the office and factory
DocuSign	Electronic Document Signing	Electronic Document Signing

Understanding the organization's dependencies on password management services like LastPass is also important. Organizations often use such services for shared passwords or employee ease of use. A breach or compromise of these services can have severe consequences for the security of sensitive data. In such cases, the cyber security team should have a clear understanding of the potential risks and be able to provide recommendations for mitigating these risks, such as implementing multi-factor authentication or changing passwords. They should also be able to perform investigations to determine if any corporate passwords are available for sale on the dark web.

Regular monitoring and reviewing service providers and their associated services and applications are crucial for proactively responding to potential privacy and security incidents and minimizing the organization's risk. By staying informed and prepared, the cyber security team can help ensure the continued security and privacy of sensitive data and systems.

Attack / Incident history and other keywords

Cybersecurity is a complex and ever-evolving field, and it is crucial to avoid potential threats. One way to achieve this is by documenting historical security events and using the information gathered to prevent similar incidents from happening in the future.

The Cyber Threat Intelligence (CTI) team plays a vital role in this process. By documenting historical security events, the CTI team can establish specific keywords and phrases that can be used to monitor for changes in the threat landscape and emerging threats that may impact the organization. This information should include details on past attacks, incidents, and other risks the organization has faced, and the CTI team should continuously monitor these keywords to identify threats proactively.

For example, if the organization has experienced a data breach in the past, and the metadata/tagging/categorization for this security event included "phishing" and "credential stealing," these keywords can be used to establish a monitoring system to detect any similar attack patterns in the future. By continuously monitoring these keywords, the CTI team can stay ahead of potential threats and take proactive measures to defend against them. Similarly, if the organization operates in the financial sector, monitoring for keywords related to financial fraud, such as "money laundering" or "credit card fraud," can help the CTI team proactively identify threats affecting the organization's industry and take appropriate action.

Historical security events can provide valuable information for the CTI team to stay ahead of potential threats and defend against cyber threats proactively. By documenting past incidents and monitoring specific keywords, the organization can take the necessary steps to raise internal awareness and defend against emerging threats effectively.

Action Items

The first step in this process is to compile a list of assets through various discovery activities. The suggested activities listed are a starting point, and the organization may choose to use additional tools, capabilities, or other means to gather the necessary information. At this stage, it may not be necessary to go into detail and identify every single asset within the organization as the Cyber Threat Intelligence (CTI) team is still in the building phase. Instead, the focus should be on sensitive assets, as they require ongoing updating and maintenance. This will ensure that the asset list remains current and accurate and that the intelligence requirements, which will be discussed in the following chapter, are met.

It is important to note that the asset list should be dynamic and subject to change, reflecting the constantly evolving nature of the cybersecurity landscape. The CTI team should regularly review and update the list to ensure that all assets are properly accounted for and that the organization is prepared to defend against potential threats.

Action items for the asset discovery process in CTI include:
- Meet with stakeholders to identify key assets, crown jewels, critical systems and technology, critical data, key brands, products, etc.
- Identify subject matter experts for various lines of business who can support the discovery initiatives.
- Identify and document physical and digital assets within the organization, including supply chain vendors and service providers.
- Identify keywords, terms, and phrases that can be used for threat monitoring.

- Identify internal data logs and sources that can be leveraged for detection capabilities and enrichment for threat intelligence services.
- Identify areas where threat intelligence can complement other security teams.
- Organize the information collected in a simple Excel or Word document or use commercial asset discovery and tracking tools.
- Leverage the information collected during the discovery process to conduct risk and threat modeling of internal assets and support the development of intelligence requirements and threat intelligence use cases.

Some simply tools can quickly help you get started such as:
- **nMap (Network Scanner):** nMap can be used to discover assets in the environment and additional information, including operating systems, IP addresses, etc. This tool could easily be used to enumerate network data as part of your asset discovery activities or frequently run to detect changes within your network quickly.
- **Corporate Website:** your corporate website has a variety of information that can be used in your asset discovery process and commonly include social media handles, addresses, domain(s), etc... By consulting your corporate website will help quickly obtain data.

- **Active Directory:** your organization's corporate domain also contains vast amounts of information that can be used for your discovery process. Typically, Active Directories can contain information about your users, their roles, and groups, as well as details regarding any domain joined system or server.
- **Helpdesk and Problem Management Systems:** These systems already include asset information at a minimum. Some of these tools also include additional modules that perform other features, which may contain asset discovery information.

Summary

When identifying assets associated with an organization or industry, it's essential to understand the business context of those assets and resources that support critical functions. This will enable organizations to prioritize efforts consistent with internal risk management strategies and business requirements. For example, an e-commerce company's critical assets may include its website, payment processing systems, and customer data. Understanding these assets and their importance to the organization's operations will help the CTI team prioritize their efforts to protect them.

The next chapter involves threat modeling of the assets identified in this chapter. This involves identifying threats that could affect the organization's assets, such as cyber-attacks, data breaches, or other malicious activities. The CTI team can develop intelligence requirements or cyber threat intelligence use cases by understanding these potential threats. Threat modeling should be an ongoing process to keep up with the latest emerging cyber threats and vulnerabilities.

Chapter #3 – Threat Modelling

Introduction

Threat modeling systematically identifies potential threats to an organization's assets, including cyber-attacks, data breaches, and other malicious activities. It provides a comprehensive understanding of the potential impact of these threats and helps prioritize allocating resources to mitigate them. In the previous chapter, we discussed the discovery of assets, which is a crucial step in starting the threat modeling process. This information serves as a foundation for threat modeling, an iterative process requiring continuous evaluation and updating as new threats emerge and the security posture evolves. Regularly conducting threat modeling activities helps organizations remain proactive and vigilant in their approach to cybersecurity.

Risk assessment and threat modelling	• Determine the risks and threats associated with corporate assets. • Model high-level threat scenarios that can impact your organization. • Categorize threat scenarios to support the development of intelligence requirements and/or use cases.
Intelligence requirements	• Leverage discovery information to determine what threats scenarios in scope. • Identify applicable sources for intelligence data. • Determine products and services the CTI team can produce to mitigate cyber threats and reduce risk. • Establish Communication Plans and SLAs

The outputs of the threat modeling process are the Intelligence Requirements, which serve as the foundation for intelligence monitoring and mitigation activities. By documenting the Intelligence Requirements, organizations can prioritize the efforts of the Cyber Threat Intelligence (CTI) team and allocate resources accordingly. It also defines the CTI products, services, and courses of action that the CTI team can produce and the stakeholders who will consume them.

In conclusion, threat modeling is a crucial aspect of a comprehensive Cyber Threat Intelligence program. It helps organizations understand the potential threats to their assets, prioritize their defenses, and allocate resources effectively. By regularly conducting threat modeling activities, organizations can remain prepared to respond to potential security threats promptly and effectively.

Chapter Objectives

In this chapter, we will focus on threat modeling to identify threat scenarios that can impact your organization and categorize these to support the development of intelligence requirements. Organizations can better prioritize their efforts and develop appropriate intelligence requirements by identifying and understanding these threats. The information gathered through threat modeling is used to prioritize the organization's efforts and allocate resources to the most at-risk areas. By staying vigilant and regularly revisiting and updating their threat models, organizations can minimize the impact of security incidents and stay protected against emerging security threats.

During this chapter, we will be going over several key concepts and activities, such as:

- Identifying threats that can impact organizational assets identified during the discovery phase.
- Modeling high-level threat scenarios to determine the assets at risk if compromised.
- Generating data-driven metrics to support the business need and requirements for a CTI program.
- Categorizing risks and threats to support the development of intelligence requirements and use cases.

For example, if your organization heavily relies on specific proprietary software for its operations. Through threat modeling, we may determine that this software is vulnerable to a particular type of cyber-attack, such as a zero-day exploit. This information can then be used to develop intelligence requirements for monitoring and proactive defense against this specific type of threat.

Threat Modelling

Threat modeling is a systematic and forward-thinking approach to enhancing an organization's cybersecurity posture. It starts with a comprehensive evaluation of all assets, including hardware, software, and data, to understand the organization's security landscape clearly. This assessment identifies potential security threats and enables a risk-based evaluation of their impact on the organization. Organizations can proactively identify, prioritize, and mitigate security risks by implementing a threat modeling framework, ultimately strengthening their defenses against cyberattacks.

Threat modeling is an iterative process that involves breaking down the assets and systems of an organization, identifying the threats they may face, and evaluating the impact of these threats. By continually revisiting and refining the threat modeling process, organizations can remain ahead of evolving threats and protect their valuable assets.

Threat Modelling can be formed in the following 3 steps:

- **Evaluate the threats:** Once you have identified your assets, you can evaluate the potential threats that could impact them. This could include data breaches, hacking attempts, insider threats, and natural disasters.

- **Evaluate the impact:** The next step is to evaluate the impact of the threats that have been identified. This will help you prioritize your defenses against cyber-attacks and determine the best action to mitigate the risks.

- **Model the threats**: Once you have evaluated the impact of the threats, you can then model the threat scenarios that could impact your assets. This will help you identify the vulnerabilities in your systems and processes and determine the best action to mitigate the risks.

Several standardized methodologies are available for threat modeling's, such as STRIDE, TRIKE, and PASTA. Using a standardized methodology, you can ensure that your threat modeling process is consistent and repeatable and that the results are consistent with industry best practices.

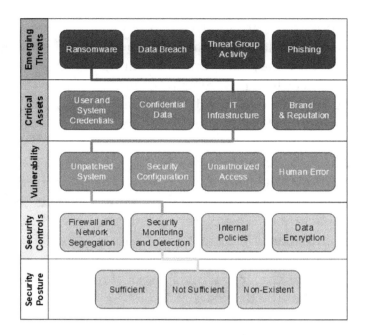

When performing your threat modeling, it is beneficial to ensure that stakeholders are involved, including IT security professionals, business leaders, and other relevant team members. This will help to ensure that all potential threats and impacts are considered and that the resulting threat model is comprehensive and relevant to the organization.

Threat modeling also helps to foster a culture of security within an organization. By involving employees in identifying and mitigating threats, organizations can educate them about the importance of security and encourage them to adopt safe practices. This helps create a security-conscious environment where everyone knows the importance of protecting sensitive information and critical systems.

Example of Threats Targeting

Organizations

Every business is vulnerable to attacks from malicious actors who seek to exploit the organization's weaknesses. These threats come in various forms and can profoundly impact an organization's operations, reputation, and financial performance.

Examples of cyber threats that organizations face include, but are not limited to:

- **Targeted attacks on the organization or industry:** Malicious campaigns aimed at obtaining sensitive information or disrupting operations.

- **Damage to Brand and Reputation:** Negative claims made with the intention of damaging an organization's brand or reputation.

- **Insider Threats:** Trusted employees performing malicious actions against the organization for personal or financial gain.

Organizations need to adopt a proactive approach to threat modeling to stay ahead of the curve and minimize the impact of these threats. This involves identifying the assets and systems critical to the organization's operations and evaluating the potential threats that could affect them. By understanding the potential impact of these threats, organizations can prioritize their defenses and develop intelligence requirements that align with their risk management strategies and business requirements.

Cyber threats are an increasingly concerning reality for all organizations. To stay informed and minimize the impact of these threats, organizations must adopt a proactive approach to threat modeling, implement robust security measures, and regularly conduct threat assessments. By doing so, organizations can protect their operations, reputation, and financial performance from the potential harm caused by cyber threats.

Critical Assets, Technologies, and Processes

Critical assets, technologies, and processes are the cornerstone of an organization's operations, and any compromise to these elements could result in severe disruptions to the organization's ability to function effectively and compete in the market.

Examples of these types of assets include but are not limited to:

Threat of Data Breach:
- **Disclosure of sensitive information can include classified data, customer information, or trade secrets:** A breach of this type of information could result in legal repercussions, loss of customer trust, and damage to the organization's reputation.
- **Disclosure of intellectual property can include patents, trademarks, and copyrights:** Compromising this type of asset could result in the loss of competitive advantage, damage to the organization's reputation, and financial loss.

Threat of Compromise:

- **The exploitation of critical and zero-day vulnerabilities:** Vulnerabilities that may suddenly emerge and, if exploited, could significantly impact the organization or its operations.
- **The exploitation of commodity malware distribution:** Distribution of commodity malware to corporate devices such as credential stealers, spam bots, backdoor Trojans, etc… that could be spying or attempting to launch a more powerful attack.

Threat of Disruption:

- **Supply-chain disruption:** The supply chain includes all the entities involved in getting a product or service to the customer, including raw materials and service providers. A disruption to the supply chain, such as a cyber-attack on a supplier, could indirectly disrupt the organization's operations.
- **Complete Loss of System (Ransomware):** Malware, when executed, encrypt a victim's computer, and may have capabilities to spread to other network devices on the network.
- **Disruption of critical systems:** These are essential to the organization's operations, such as power systems, transportation systems, and communication systems. A disruption to these systems could result in significant operational disruption, loss of revenue, and damage to the organization's reputation.

These assets are the backbone of an organization's operations, and any compromise to them could result in severe consequences, including disruptions to operations, damage to reputation, and financial losses.

To ensure the protection of these assets, it is crucial to conduct a thorough threat assessment. This involves identifying potential threats and assessing the impact they could have on the organization if they were to materialize. The outcome of this assessment should be a comprehensive understanding of the threats posed to the organization and its critical assets.

Technology Stack

Companies increasingly rely on technology to carry out their day-to-day operations. They must be aware of cyber threats that can potentially target their technical infrastructure. The more technical devices an organization utilizes, the larger the surface area becomes for potential malicious actors to exploit. Any minor vulnerability in a technical device, if successfully targeted, could result in unauthorized or undesired activities, which could eventually lead to serious security breaches. These threats can range from simple disruptions to operations to more advanced attacks that can steal confidential information. As a cyber security professional, it is essential to constantly educate organizations on the importance of being proactive in identifying and mitigating these potential threats.

Examples of these types of threats include, but are not limited to:

Threat of Data Breach:
- Disclosure of sensitive information or intellectual property: Weaknesses within security systems could be exploited to expose classified information.

Threat of Compromise:
- **Critical and zero-day vulnerabilities:** Vulnerabilities that may suddenly emerge and, if exploited, could significantly impact the organization or its operations.

- **Unauthorized Access:** Access gained to a system or application through unauthorized means (hacked).

Threat of Disruption:
- **Loss of availability (DDoS):** DDoS attack aims to disrupt an organization's operations by overwhelming its systems with traffic. This can cause the systems to crash, resulting in a loss of service for legitimate users.
- **Ransomware:** Malware, when executed, encrypt a victim's computer, and may have capabilities to spread to other network devices on the network.
- **Disruption to critical systems:** Weaknesses within critical systems could lead to significant disruption for the organization and disruption in the supply chain. For example, attacks or disruption to raw product as or service providers could indirectly disrupt an organization's operations.

It is vital to comprehend your organization's technology infrastructure and identify potential vulnerabilities in those assets. By staying abreast of the newest security threats and adopting a proactive stance towards threat modeling, organizations can effectively mitigate the consequences of these threats on their daily operations, reputation, and overall financial stability.

Corporate domains/website

As a cyber security professional, it's crucial to understand the potential risks that a registered website or domain can pose to an organization. Every organization has at least one domain; in some cases, multiple domains are used for various purposes, such as legacy names, product promotions, related events, etc. Malicious actors can exploit these domain names through typo-squatting or substitution attacks. In these attacks, the attacker will register a domain name like the legitimate domain, making it difficult for employees or clients to differentiate between the two.

Threat of Compromise:
- Phishing Targeting Employees: Spoofed websites or domains attempt to obtain the credentials of employees, or spoof email addresses and request specific actions of other employees.

Reputational Threats:
- Phishing Targeting Clients: Spoofed websites domains attempting to collect the login credentials of your clients.

Another potential threat against your corporate domain is the compromise of Domain Name System (DNS) servers or registrars, a serious security risk that could significantly impact your domain and website. As a cornerstone of the internet infrastructure, the DNS is responsible for translating domain names into IP addresses, enabling users to access websites using a domain name instead of an IP address.

Organizations must stay informed of the latest security threats and take a proactive approach to threat modeling to minimize the impact of these types of threats on their operations, reputation, and financial stability. Organizations should develop a comprehensive threat modeling program that considers the various threats affecting their domains and websites.

Understanding the types of threats affecting corporate domains is crucial in developing a comprehensive threat modeling program. By staying informed of the latest threats and taking a proactive approach to threat modeling, organizations can minimize the impact of these types of threats on their operations, reputation, and bottom line. Remember that the examples provided are just a few possible ways attackers can use corporate domains as an attack vector. It is essential always to be vigilant and stay informed of the latest threat trends.

Organizations Leadership

As technology continues to evolve, so do the methods used by cybercriminals to attack organizations. One increasingly popular tactic is targeting the social media accounts of key individuals within an organization, such as executives and leadership team members.

One of the most common forms of attack is impersonation, where the attacker creates a fake profile posing as a well-known individual, and tricks others into sending them money or sensitive information. This type of attack is particularly dangerous because it leverages people's trust in well-known figures, often creating a sense of urgency that pressures the victim into acting quickly without verifying the message's authenticity.

Examples of these types of threats include but are not limited to:

Reputational Threats:
- **Spoofed Social Media Accounts:**
  - **Scams and Misinformation:** Posting information that is incorrect, harmful, or otherwise not in line with the official corporate message. This situation could result in an adverse impact on the official organization's reputation.
  - **Pre-Texting:** Leveraging a spoofed account to initiate a conversation with a legitimate connection with malicious intent/purposes.

Financial Threats:
- **Business Email Compromise (BEC):** Targeting sensitive individuals within the accounting department to pay fake or otherwise modified invoices.

Threat of Compromise:
- **Credential Phishing:** Attempts to obtain credentials of a sensitive individual to gain access to sensitive information.
- **Whaling:** Targeting a company's executive or upper management positions to obtain sensitive information or request specific actions of other individuals (i.e., purchase iTunes Gift Cards).

These are just a few examples of the types of threats that organizations may face when targeting their leadership. Organizations need to be aware of these threats and take steps to protect their key individuals and leaders. By understanding these tactics, organizations can better protect themselves from these attacks.

Targeting the social media accounts of key individuals within an organization can be a highly effective tactic for cybercriminals. Organizations need to be aware of the risks and take steps to protect themselves, their leaders, and their sensitive information. By remaining vigilant and taking proactive measures, organizations can minimize their risk and help to defend against these types of cyber threats.

Social Media

Social media has become crucial for companies to communicate with their customers, increase their visibility, and build their brands. However, with businesses' widespread use of social media, the risk of cyber threats targeting these accounts has also grown.

Cybercriminals constantly seek new ways to exploit vulnerabilities in an organization's digital infrastructure. In the case of social media, these threats can take many forms, from hacking into an organization's social media account to stealing sensitive information or posting malicious content to damaging the company's reputation. They can also launch phishing attacks, spread malware, or impersonate the company's social media accounts to trick users into giving away sensitive information.

There are many threats, tactics, and techniques that threat actors could use to leverage your brand via spoofed accounts for malicious intent, including but not limited to the following:

Reputational Threats:

- **Scams and Misinformation:** Posting information that is incorrect, harmful, or otherwise not in line with the official corporate message. This situation could result in a negative impact on the official organization's reputation.

- **Malware delivery:** Spoofed accounts post messages and links to malicious sites with the intent to deliver malware.

- **Promotion of Counterfeit Products:** Promotion of products like a legitimate company or organization yet are heavily discounted and counterfeit.

- **Fake Websites:** Promotion of products or services that redirect to a fake website with the primary intent of stealing payment card information.

Organizations must be aware of these threats and implement proper controls and procedures to protect their social media presence. This includes monitoring for and reporting any suspicious activity, implementing two-factor authentication for all social media accounts, and regularly updating passwords. By taking these steps, organizations can better protect themselves from these types of threats and minimize the potential impact on their reputation and financial losses.

Supply-Chain

Organizations in today's interconnected world rely on a complex network of service providers and vendors to support their operations. As a cyber security professional, it is essential to understand the potential risks associated with organizations working with service providers and vendors. These third-party entities can pose significant security threats, including data breaches and unauthorized access to sensitive information.

In the event your service provider/vendor or supply chain is affected by a cyber threat, this could also impact your organization and or operations as well in the form of:

Availability Threats:
- **Denial of Service:** If a service provider is unavailable, this may disrupt your organization.

Threat of Data Breaches:
- **Information Disclosure:** If a service provider has been compromised, this may result in the disclosure of your organization's sensitive information.

Threat of Compromise:
- **Supply-Chain Malware Delivery:** Supply-Chain software and services installed within your organization could pose risks in the event a malicious update has been pushed. (i.e., M.E. Docs and Kaseya were both software providers that were compromised and pushed a malicious update resulting in ransomware distribution.

Organizations must take a proactive stance in identifying and addressing supply-chain cyber threats, which pose a significant risk to their operations. This requires regular risk assessments of their service providers and vendors to understand the threats that can affect them.

Adopting a comprehensive and holistic approach to cyber security is crucial for protecting against supply-chain cyber threats. This approach focuses on securing the organization's infrastructure and the entire supply chain, including vendors and service providers. By taking these proactive steps, organizations can protect their operations, minimize the impact of cyber-attacks, and ensure that they can continue to operate smoothly and effectively.

Threat Metrics

Utilizing threat metrics provides organizations with a visual representation of the types and nature of cyber threats, making it easier to understand and prioritize the risks. This information is also essential in supporting the development of the organization's CTI Intelligence Requirements, which outline the specific knowledge and data needed to manage the risks. By using cyber threat metrics, organizations can gain valuable insights into the threats that pose the most significant risk to their operations and assets. This allows them to tailor their CTI program to address their organization's unique needs and vulnerabilities.

Threats Affecting the Organization

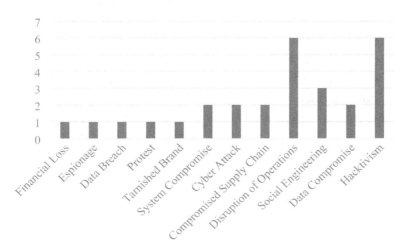

One of the critical benefits of these metrics is that they can serve as a compelling argument for the implementation of a Cyber Threat Intelligence (CTI) program within an organization. By presenting data-driven metrics that highlight the organization's current vulnerabilities and the potential risks posed by cyber threats, it's possible to convince executive leadership of the need for a CTI program. This not only helps to secure the necessary funding and resources to establish and maintain a CTI program but also ensures that the program is effectively implemented to protect the organization from cyber-attacks.

However, it's crucial to be mindful of the metrics being used. When developing these metrics, it's essential to make sure they align with the specific needs and requirements of the organization. This is crucial when seeking support from executive leadership, as we need to demonstrate the justification for investment in cyber security measures and the potential impact of cyber threats on the organization. By presenting data-driven metrics that are specific to the organization and its intelligence requirements, we can effectively build a case for a robust CTI program.

Action items

From the assets identified during the "Discovery" chapter, perform threat modeling activities to identify the various threats. Feel free to conduct additional discovery activities through other tools, capabilities, or other means to collect needed information. As the CTI is still in the building phase, it may not be required to go overly in-depth to identify every asset within the organization.

Getting started with threat modeling can be broken down into the follow steps:

- **Define your scope:** Depending on the size of your organization, start by identifying the assets that are critical to your organization, such as data, systems, and infrastructure. This will help you understand what needs to be protected and where potential vulnerabilities may lie.

- **Identify potential threats:** Identify potential threats that could impact your assets and systems. This could include external threats like hackers or internal threats like employees.

- **Understand how these threats can be realized:** Based on the threats identified, start to conceptualize how these threats can be realized, including the steps a threat actor would need to take.

- **Assess and rate the risk:** Assess the risk associated with each threat by placing the likelihood of it occurring and the potential impact it could have on your assets and your overall organization.

- **Document your threat models:** Document the threat models and their associated assets in a structured form or format. These will be referenced and referred to in future chapters as well as over the life of your CTI Team. These will also be used as the fundamental basis of your Intelligence Requirements.

- **Categorizing and grouping your threats:** By categorizing and grouping your threats into different classifications, you will start to visualize the connections and begin to see the clusters of assets and similar scenarios that could be affected by similar threats.

- **Develop metrics:** Based on your documented threat models, their categorizations, and ratings, develop some simple threat metrics that will support your Intelligence Requirement and can also be used to support your business case for a Cyber Threat Intelligence program.

Some assets may be associated with multiple threats, while others, particularly those with lower sensitivity, may not pose any significant threat. This is a common occurrence, and it's essential to focus on securing the assets that are most critical to the organization and have the most significant potential to cause harm.

Summary

This chapter focuses on conducting a thorough threat modeling exercise to identify these threats. By doing so, organizations can gain valuable insights into the scenarios that may pose a risk to their operations and develop targeted intelligence requirements accordingly.

A clear understanding of the potential threats and corresponding intelligence requirements is the key to implementing effective threat detection, monitoring, and mitigation strategies. These intelligence requirements are the foundation for developing a comprehensive cyber threat intelligence (CTI) program. By formalizing these requirements, organizations can prioritize their CTI efforts and allocate resources to the areas that need the most attention.

Chapter #4 – Intelligence Requirements (IR)

Chapter #4a – IR Definition

Introduction

In this chapter, we will delve into the process of defining intelligence requirements for the CTI program, which serves as a foundation and roadmap for the CTI team's efforts. Intelligence requirements are a prioritized list of information needs that the CTI team must gather, process, analyze and disseminate to support the organization's cyber defense efforts. They are crucial for ensuring the CTI team focuses on the most critical and relevant threat information. By clearly defining these requirements, the CTI team can save time and resources by avoiding collecting irrelevant or redundant data, which could result in a disorganized and ineffective CTI program.

The previous threat modeling activities are crucial in determining the intelligence requirements. We will identify key threat scenarios that could impact the organization and categorize them based on potential impact, severity, and likelihood. This will inform the prioritization of the intelligence requirements, ensuring that the CTI team focuses on the organization's most critical threats and risks.

Intelligence requirements	• Leverage discovery information to determine what threats scenarios in scope. • Identify applicable sources for intelligence data. • Determine products and services the CTI team can produce to mitigate cyber threats and reduce risk. • Establish Communication Plans and SLAs
Intelligence tools	• Determine tools to collect, store, & process data. • Understand how various intelligence tools can integrate with each other as well as other security tools, or data sources. • Determine technical dependencies to support CTI tools.

Once the intelligence requirements have been defined, we will determine the necessary intelligence sources, tools, and technical dependencies to support the CTI program. This involves selecting data collection and storage methods, integrating intelligence tools, and the identification of other security tools or data sources that may be required.

Developing a list of intelligence requirements for a CTI program is crucial in establishing a successful CTI program. By defining these requirements, the CTI team can ensure that its efforts are focused on the most relevant and critical threat information, thereby reducing the overall cyber risk for the organization.

Chapter Objectives

In this chapter, we will use the threat modeling activities from the previous chapter to create a comprehensive list of intelligence requirements for effective cybersecurity. We can develop intelligence about attacker methods, tools, motivations, and tactics by understanding potential threats and vulnerabilities. This information will inform our threat mitigation strategies and help protect an organization's assets.

Throughout this chapter, you will learn how to leverage threat modeling information from the previous chapter to:

- Leverage discovery information to establish threat scenarios that could impact your organization.
- Identify potential threat scenarios that affect their organization and prioritize the most critical ones.
- Determine which threat scenarios can be monitored and responded to proactively.
- Categorize the threat scenarios into groups based on their potential impact, severity, and likelihood.

Defining intelligence requirements is a crucial step for the success of a Cyber Threat Intelligence program as it sets the foundation for the CTI team to collect, analyze, and disseminate relevant threat information. By the end of the chapter, participants should understand the requirements and be able to support the organization in reducing cyber risks and mitigating threats. A well-defined intelligence requirement process leads to a comprehensive and effective CTI program.

Intelligence Requirements Definition

Intelligence requirements

A well-designed Cyber Threat Intelligence (CTI) program relies on a comprehensive set of intelligence requirements to guide the CTI team in gathering, analyzing, and disseminating threat information. These requirements are derived from prior threat modeling efforts and are tailored to specific organizational scenarios to provide context and relevance to the potential impact of the threats. In essence, the intelligence requirements form the foundation for effective CTI operations and support informed decision-making in the face of evolving cybersecurity threats.

Examples of intelligence requirements include:

- What new vulnerabilities have been discovered that have the potential to affect the organization's technology stack?
- Have any fake social media profiles been created to impersonate the organization's brand or its sensitive employees?
- Which cyber threats actively target the industry or geographic region in which the organization operates?
- What is the modus operandi of specific threat actors known to target the organization in the past?

Defining the intelligence requirements for a CTI program is a critical step in determining the scope of potential threat scenarios, identifying sources of relevant intelligence data, and developing plans for collecting and analyzing this data. This phase also involves establishing clear communication protocols, defining service-level agreements, and identifying necessary tools and technical dependencies to support the CTI program.

The purpose of establishing these intelligence requirements is to give organizations a clear understanding of the types of threats they face and to help them develop effective strategies to defend against them. The description of these requirements should be precise and unambiguous, clearly outlining the types of threats the organization is trying to detect, defend and mitigate against.

For example, organizations may have many types of phishing intelligence requirements, such as:

- **Credential phishing targeting employees:** This involves threat actors pretending to be trustworthy to obtain employees' login credentials. An example could be a phishing email pretending to be from the company's IT department, asking employees to reset their passwords.

- **Credential phishing targeting customers:** This involves threat actors impersonating a reputable organization, such as a bank or an e-commerce website, to obtain customers' login credentials. An example could be an email appearing to be from a well-known online retailer asking customers to reset their password.

- **Spam delivery of commodity malware:** This involves sending unsolicited emails containing malware, such as Trojans, spyware, or information stealers, to infect the recipient's device.

- **Spam delivery of ransomware:** This involves sending unsolicited emails containing ransomware to infect the recipient's device and encrypt their data until a ransom is paid.

When defining intelligence requirements, organizations should develop requirements that answer questions such as "What are we looking for?" and "How badly are we affected?" They should also specify a priority field, indicating whether the intelligence requirement is of high, medium, or low priority. A categorization field helps to classify the intelligence requirement, and a frequency field indicates how often the intelligence requirement should be performed.

Phishing campaigns, for example, may have an intelligence requirement to identify phishing campaigns that are used to compromise the credentials of employees. The priority is high, indicating the significance of this threat. The categorization is "credential phishing," and the frequency is daily, indicating that this requirement should be checked daily. The description should specify the objective of the phishing campaign, such as "to identify phishing campaigns that have the threat actor's objective of obtaining employees' credentials to gain access to the corporate environment.

Intelligence Requirements could include the following:
- Monitoring for phishing campaigns attempting to obtain the credentials of employees.
- Determining if identified phishing campaigns are targeting the company directly or are part of a mass spamming campaign.

- Identifying indicators of compromise that can be used for threat-hunting activities and for integrating detection and prevention capabilities within the organization's security tools.
- We are identifying employees who have fallen victim to a phishing campaign to understand the extent of the attack and support the security investigation.

By having clearly defined intelligence requirements, organizations can better identify and defend against threats and minimize the impact of successful attacks.

Anatomy of an Intelligence Requirement

Defining Intelligence Requirements (IR) is vital for building a comprehensive Cyber Threat Intelligence (CTI) program. The IR document outlines the specific cyber threats faced by the organization, the objectives and priorities of the CTI program, and the desired outcomes. This helps prioritize the organization's efforts, allocate resources effectively, and align the CTI program with the security strategy. The IR document ensures a targeted, coordinated, and practical approach to cyber security, making it crucial for the success of the CTI program.

An example of a formalized and documented intelligence requirement might include the following sections:

- **Definition:** This section describes the higher-level risk the organization is trying to defend against and provides more granular details of the specific threats associated with that risk. For example, the definition might be "phishing attempts," and the threat description could be "phishing attempts targeting our clients." Another example might be "phishing attempts to gain credentials to Office 365."

- **Intelligence Requirements:** This section lists the specific data or information the organization is trying to find and obtain. This might include "our credentials for our organization being sold on the Dark Web" or "what type of campaigns are being used to target our clients."

- **Collection Plans and Intelligence Sources:** This section describes the data sources that will be used to obtain the information needed to meet the intelligence requirements. This might include internal data sources, open-source information, social media, or commercial tools.

- **Intelligence Products, Service Level Agreements, and Communication Plans:** This section describes what will be produced, how it will be produced, who will receive it, and what the product will be. It also outlines the service level agreements for delivering the intelligence, such as a flash report with a 4-hour response time in the case of an emerging threat.

- **Courses of Action**: This section outlines the actions and activities that will be taken to help defend the organization against the identified threats. This includes using IOCs to search for malicious software, taking down phishing sites, etc.

IR – 1 - Threat			
Description:			

IR-1b: Threat						
Priority:		**Category:**			**Frequency:**	
Description:						
Intelligence Requirements (IRs):						
•						
Collection Plans:						
Internal:	•					
Open Source:	•					
Social Media:	•					
Commercial:	•					

Service Catalogue:

	Products:	Recipients:	SLAs:
Strategic:	•	•	•
Operational:	•	•	•
Tactical:	•	•	•
Technical:	•	•	•

Summary of Activities:	

Risk Reducing Courses of Action (CoAs):	
Discover:	•
Detect:	•
Deny:	•
Disrupt:	•
Degrade:	•
Deceive:	•
Destroy:	•

For example, we may have multiple types of phishing intelligence requirements:

- Credential phishing targeting employee's (i.e. O365)
- Credential phishing targeting customers (i.e. Spotify, Coin Base, etc...)
- Spam delivery:
  - commodity malware
  - ransomware

IR 1 – Phishing Campaigns
Identification of phishing campaigns that have the ability to spread malicious software or compromise the credentials of our employees, or customers.

IR-1b: Credential Phishing Targeting Internal Employees					
Priority:	High	**Category:**	Credential Phishing	**Frequency:**	Daily
Description:					
Identify phishing campaigns where the threat actor's objective is to obtain credentials of our employees in order to gain access to our corporate environment.					

Other parts of the definition section include the following:

- A priority field to indicate whether this is a high, medium, or low priority IR.
- A categorization field to help classify/tag what type of IR this is associated with.
- A frequency field to indicate how often this Intelligence Requirement should be performed.

IR 1 – Phishing Campaigns
Identification of phishing campaigns that have the ability to spread malicious software or compromise the credentials of our employees, or customers.

IR-1b: Credential Phishing Targeting Internal Employees					
Priority:	High	Category:	Credential Phishing	Frequency:	Daily
Description:					
Identify phishing campaigns where the threat actor's objective is to obtain credentials of our employees in order to gain access to our corporate environment.					
Intelligence Requirements (IRs):					
• Monitor for phishing campaigns that are attempting to obtain the credentials of our employees. • Determine if identified phishing campaigns are targeting our company directly or via mass "spray-and-prey" technique. • Identify IOCs that can be used for threat hunting activities as well as detection/prevention capabilities within corporate security tools. • Identify which and how many employees may have fallen victim.					

The following chapters will address many steps and aspects to consider when creating intelligence requirements for each component.

Defining intelligence requirements is critical to building a Cyber Threat Intelligence program and requires careful consideration of each of these sections. The following chapters will focus on each area of the intelligence requirements in more detail, including but not limited to collection plans, intelligence products, and courses of action.

Sample intelligence Requirements Definitions

Brand and Asset

Identifying brand and asset threats is one of the most important aspects of these intelligence requirements. This involves understanding the types of attacks that pose a risk to the organization and the methods malicious actors use to carry out these attacks. The information collected during this process informs the development of the CTI program and is used to guide the collection and analysis of threat intelligence.

Examples of these threats include but are not limited to:

- **Direct Threats to Brand or Physical Assets:** This intelligence requirement focuses on monitoring the brand to promptly identify any negative mentions or activities that may harm the brand's reputation or cause physical damage to the organization's assets. For example, tracking mentions of the organization on social media to detect potential cyber-attacks or physical threats to the organization's facilities.

- **Brand or Product Mentions on Sensitive Sources:** This involves monitoring brand mentions from sources typically associated with malicious activity or threat actors, such as the dark web, Reddit forums, or Facebook groups. For example, tracking mentions of the organization's brand on criminal forums to detect potential data breaches or intellectual property theft.

- **Protest and Activism with Potential to Impact Operations:** This intelligence requirement identifies protests and activism that may directly or indirectly impact the organization's operations, such as disrupting operations, causing damage, or other harm. For example, tracking news and social media posts related to protests and activism near the organization's facilities to detect potential threats to the operations.

- **Corporate and Executive Monitoring:** This involves monitoring negative mentions or online activity directed towards executives, such as fake social media accounts, negative posts by employees or customers, and comments by executives that may be taken out of context or perceived as unfavorable. For example, tracking mentions of the organization's CEO on social media to detect potential risks to the organization's reputation or potential insider threats.

- **Sensitive Images or Mentions Originating from Classified Locations:** The objective of this intelligence requirement is to identify the public disclosure of sensitive information, such as images or mentions from within an organization's sensitive locations, such as manufacturing facilities, data centers, or employee desks. For example, tracking mentions of the organization's confidential information on social media to detect potential data leaks or security breaches.

- **Malicious App Stores:** This involves monitoring third-party app stores to identify non-authentic and republished mobile applications, for example, tracking third-party app stores for republished versions of the organization's mobile applications that may contain malicious code and monitoring app store reviews to detect potential security vulnerabilities or customer complaints.

Clear and specific intelligence requirements are essential for a successful Cyber Threat Intelligence (CTI) program. These requirements provide a roadmap for the CTI team to gather and analyze relevant information to defend against cyber threats. They should be tailored to the unique needs and challenges of the organization and its industry. The focus of the intelligence requirements should be on monitoring and identifying brand and asset threats to the organization's reputation, brand image, and critical assets such as intellectual property and sensitive information. Thorough monitoring and identification of these threats are crucial for the continued success and resilience of the organization against cyber-attacks.

Threats Associated with the Technology Stack.

As a CTI Team, keeping a close eye on any threats associated with your organization's technology stack is crucial. This includes monitoring for any leaks or disclosures of confidential information, which can significantly affect an organization's security operations and trade secrets. Identifying and assessing any potential vulnerabilities in the technology stack is essential, as they can also impact the organization's overall security. By proactively monitoring for these threats, a cyber security team can take necessary measures to remediate identified risks and ensure the safety and security of the technology infrastructure.

- **Confidential Information Leaks:** This could be the disclosure of sensitive data, such as credentials, database dumps, or other types of documentation, that has the potential to impact security operations and trade secrets. For example, the CTI team may monitor the dark web for leaked credentials and proactively remediate identified risks.

- **Mentions of IP Addresses and Infrastructure on Sensitive Sources:** CTI can monitor sensitive sources, such as forums or websites associated with malicious activity, to identify IP addresses and infrastructure observations. By assessing the goals and objectives of threat actors associated with these mentions, the CTI team can use the information for further action, such as mitigating botnet activity associated with the organization's IP addresses.

- **Vulnerabilities with Potential to Impact the Technology Stack:** CTI can monitor for vulnerabilities in the technology stack and provide a risk-based assessment of their potential impact. For example, the CTI team may monitor for threat actors exploiting zero-day vulnerabilities in technology appliances or assets within the environment and provide recommendations for remediation controls.

These intelligence requirements are to monitor and proactively identify potential risks and impacts to the technology stack and to provide remediation recommendations to mitigate these risks.

Threats Targeting Organizations, Industry or Business Operations

One of the critical objectives of a CTI program is to stay informed about the overall cyber-threat landscape, including threats targeting your organization, industry, and business operations. This involves gathering, analyzing, and using relevant threat intelligence capabilities to identify potential threats that can impact your organization. This information can help the CTI team identify potential attack vectors and proactively implement detection and mitigation controls to protect against similar attacks in the future proactively.

- **Industry peers targeted in cyber-attacks**: By monitoring industry peers, the CTI team can gain insight into common attack vectors and tactics, techniques, and procedures (TTPs) used by threat actors. This information can be used to implement controls and detections to defend against similar attacks proactively. For example, suppose an industry peer reports a targeted attack involving a specific type of malware. In that case, the CTI team can monitor for that type of malware and implement controls to prevent a similar attack from occurring in their organization.

- **Supply-chain threats:** The CTI team must monitor the supply chain for potential threats that may be delivered through side-channel attacks. For example, the SolarWinds and MeDoc incidents demonstrate the importance of monitoring the supply chain to prevent the delivery of compromised software updates. The CTI team should regularly assess products and services from vendors to ensure they are safe and secure inputs and outputs for the organization.

- **Phishing campaigns delivering commodity malware:** Phishing campaigns are often used to provide commodity malware and must be monitored by the CTI team. The CTI program must identify various indicators of compromise (IOCs) and design blocking controls to prevent the distribution and potential exploitation of zero-day vulnerabilities in the wild. Intelligence derived from monitoring zero-day vulnerabilities can be used to identify attacks and assess the overall business impact.

- **Infrastructure actively targeted by sophisticated advanced persistent threats (APTs):** The CTI program must monitor emerging threats actively targeting infrastructure to identify imminent cyberattacks and threat actors.

Adequate protection against cyber threats requires a deep understanding of the Tactics, Techniques, and Procedures (TTPs) utilized by threat actors. By staying abreast of these TTPs, the Cyber Threat Intelligence (CTI) team can proactively defend against potential attacks. For instance, if the CTI team identifies an Advanced Persistent Threat (APT) campaign targeting a specific infrastructure, they can deploy countermeasures to mitigate the risk of a successful attack.

Emerging Cyber Threats

The Cyber Threat Intelligence (CTI) team monitors and tracks the evolving threat landscape to protect an organization from cyber threats. The team closely monitors for newly detected malware, updates, and modifications to known malware, sensitive sources for new malware developments, zero-day vulnerabilities, and new and trending vulnerabilities. By doing so, the CTI team can understand these threats' functions, behaviors, and potential impacts, identify, and implement adequate controls to prevent exploitation, and stay ahead of the curve in the face of rapidly evolving cyber threats.

The CTI team also assesses the potential risk to the organization's environment and technology stack and takes necessary measures to mitigate the threat. By tracking new and trending vulnerabilities, the team stays up to date with the latest threat landscape and understands the impact, infection vectors, and potential consequences if these vulnerabilities were to be exploited. The CTI team's continuous monitoring and tracking of the threat landscape enables it to proactively implement mitigation controls and ensure the security of the organization's technology stack.

This includes monitoring for:

- **New malware:** By tracking newly discovered malware, the CTI team gains insight into its functions, behaviors, and potential impacts. The team can identify and implement controls to prevent the exploitation of this information.

- **Updates to known malware:** Monitoring changes to existing malware strains allows the CTI team to stay up to date on new functions and behaviors, allowing for more effective mitigation strategies.

- **Sensitive sources:** Keeping an eye on sensitive sources for new malware developments provides the CTI team with a deeper understanding of how the malware operates and threat actors' intentions.

- **Zero-day vulnerabilities:** Monitoring for zero-day vulnerabilities helps the CTI team quickly identify and respond to exploiting newly discovered vulnerabilities that could affect the organization.

- **New and trending vulnerabilities:** Tracking new and trending vulnerabilities is critical in understanding the landscape of the threat, potential impacts, and infection vectors.

The goal of the CTI team is to provide the organization with the necessary tools and knowledge to defend itself against cyber-attacks and respond effectively in the event of a breach. A comprehensive CTI program that includes monitoring for emerging threats and newly identified malware helps organizations stay ahead of the curve and remain protected against the ever-evolving cyber threat landscape.

Threat Actor Activity

The CTI team is also responsible for regularly monitoring the activity of known and emerging threat actors to maintain a robust Cyber Threat Intelligence (CTI) program. This monitoring process aims to track the behaviors, techniques, and targets of these actors and groups. This information helps us understand the evolution of their tactics and the industries, organizations, and sectors they focus on, enabling us to evaluate our defenses' preparedness against these threats.

The CTI team uses this information to stay ahead of the curve by detecting new tactics, techniques, and procedures (TTPs) used by these actors. We then assess the effectiveness of our existing security controls and make necessary modifications to improve the organization's overall security posture. This proactive approach helps us anticipate and defend against potential cyber-attacks and respond more effectively in case of any incidents.

This includes monitoring includes but is not limited to:

- **Monitoring Specific Threat Actors/Groups:** This involves tracking and monitoring events related to identifying specific threat actors or groups. It helps the CTI team stay informed about these actors' latest developments and activities.

- **Identifying Targeted Organizations, Industries, and Sectors:** By monitoring threat actor activity, the CTI team can determine the organizations, industries, and sectors targeted by the actors. This information can be used to prioritize the organization's defense and allocate resources accordingly.

- **New TTPs Identification:** The CTI team monitors threat actor activity to identify new TTPs used by these actors. This allows the CTI team to continuously improve the organization's defense by integrating new controls and detection capabilities into security tools.

- **Indicators of Compromise (IOCs) Identification:** The CTI team monitors for new threat actor activity to identify new IOCs. These IOCs provide early warning signs of a potential attack and allow the CTI team to take proactive measures to defend the organization.

Monitoring threat actor activity is crucial to a comprehensive threat intelligence (CTI) program. By continuously gathering and analyzing data, the CTI team can stay informed on threats' latest tactics and tools, prioritize their defense efforts, allocate resources effectively, and proactively protect the organization from future attacks. This proactive approach helps reduce the risk of successful attacks and protects sensitive data and assets critical to the business's success.

Action Items

To build a Cyber Threat Intelligence (CTI) program, it is crucial to identify the most critical findings from previous risk assessments and threat controls. Group these findings into categories and subcategories and clearly define the risks and threats they pose. Compile intelligence requirements for each category and subcategory, keeping the organization's capabilities in mind. Ensure that each intelligence requirement is specific, and its output is in the form of strategic, operational, tactical, or technical measures such as mitigation of cyber threats or enhancements to existing controls.

Action items to start defining your Intelligence Requirements:
- Based on intelligence sources, determine what tools are best suited to collect information from these sources.
- Determine the tools needed for threat events, IOC, and COA tracking.
- Compare and contrast various tools with similar capabilities to find appropriate tools for your requirements.
    - Could open-source versions of commercial tools work just as well?
    - Do other tools support automation and integrations?
- Understand the requirements and dependencies to use and support these tools (i.e., licensing costs, hardware/software resources, maintenance costs, support, etc...)
- Determine where these tools will live, how they will be set up, and how they will be accessed.
    - Could custom scripting (i.e., Bash / PowerShell / Python) be used for additional automation and batch processing (either now or in the future)

- Establish your operational security requirements and what is required to support these (i.e., VPN services, dedicated/segregated network, and hardware).
- Evaluate the costs associated with performing specific intelligence requirements and determine if they are cost-effective (risk vs. reward).
- If costs are too high vs. the potential reward, performing specific intelligence requirements may not be feasible. In this event, you have three choices:
  - Drop the intelligence requirement altogether.
  - Outsource IR to an intelligence vendor.
  - Scope down the original intelligence requirement until it fits a suitable cost range while still being effective as an IR.
- Update the intelligence requirements to reflect any updates or changes as you evaluate your tools (i.e., sources may change, additional COAs due to enhanced tool capabilities and changes in the IR objective).

A successful CTI program must balance budget and technology to provide valuable insights, and as it matures, it can upgrade its tools and capabilities to stay relevant and effective against evolving cyber threats.

Summary

This chapter discussed the definition of intelligence requirements based on the threat modeling activities performed in the previous chapter. By defining intelligence requirements, organizations can prioritize its threat intelligence efforts and focus on the most critical threats and risks, ensuring that the CTI team can respond proactively to threats and reduce overall cyber risk.

The next chapter focuses on building knowledge and skills for a practical Cyber Threat Intelligence (CTI) program. It will cover three key areas:

- Identifying and evaluating intelligence sources
- Establishing collection objectives and capabilities
- Determining intelligence tooling dependencies

By the end of the following chapter, participants will be able to understand the value of different intelligence sources, determine specific data sources and collection plans, and estimate the costs of intelligence tooling dependencies. They will be equipped with the necessary knowledge and skills to effectively operationalize their intelligence requirements and build a robust CTI program to support their organization in reducing cyber risks and potentially mitigating threats.

Chapter #4b – IR - Intelligence Sources and Collection Plans

Introduction

The Intelligence Requirements phase of cyber security is crucial in establishing an effective threat intelligence program for an organization. This phase focuses on identifying and collecting the critical data sources that will support the organization's intelligence goals and objectives. The Cyber Threat Intelligence (CTI) team is responsible for evaluating various options for sourcing and collecting threat intelligence to determine the most effective methods that consider both internal and external sources of information.

The first step in the Intelligence Requirements phase involves using the information gathered in the Discovery phase to define the in-scope threat scenarios. The CTI team then identifies relevant intelligence data sources, determines the CTI products, and services that can mitigate cyber threats and reduce risk, and establishes communication plans and service level agreements (SLAs) to ensure a smooth flow of information.

Intelligence requirements	• Leverage discovery information to determine what threats scenarios in scope. • Identify applicable sources for intelligence data. • Determine products and services the CTI team can produce to mitigate cyber threats and reduce risk. • Establish Communication Plans and SLAs
Intelligence tools	• Determine tools to collect, store, & process data. • Understand how various intelligence tools can integrate with each other as well as other security tools, or data sources. • Determine technical dependencies to support CTI tools.

The CTI team determines the tools needed for collecting, storing, and processing the data in the Intelligence Tools phase. They evaluate how the intelligence tools can integrate with other security tools or data sources and assess any technical dependencies required to support CTI tools.

Examples of data sources that can be included in a CTI collection plan include internal data repositories, open-source intelligence, commercial intelligence portals and services, and industry organizations. This phase aims to provide a comprehensive understanding of identifying, evaluating, and implementing effective collection plans that support the organization's intelligence requirements.

By the end of the Intelligence Requirements phase, participants should clearly understand the threat intelligence sources, data collection methods, and the objectives and capabilities necessary to support the threat intelligence program. This phase sets the foundation for a robust and effective threat intelligence program that can help organizations stay ahead of cyber threats and maintain the security of their systems and data.

Chapter Objectives

This chapter aims to provide participants with a comprehensive understanding of the key skills required for building an effective CTI program. One of the first and most important steps is identifying and evaluating various intelligence sources. This includes understanding the strengths and weaknesses of different sources and their reliability and relevance to the organization's specific needs.

Establishing clear collection objectives and capabilities is crucial to leverage these sources effectively. This involves determining the specific information required to support the organization's goals and how this information will be collected and analyzed. This can involve utilizing various techniques, such as network and endpoint monitoring, open-source intelligence gathering, and social media analysis.

Upon completion of this chapter, participants will be equipped with the necessary knowledge and skills to effectively build a robust Cyber Threat Intelligence (CTI) program and be able to:

- **Identify and Evaluate Intelligent Sources:** Participants will be able to recognize the various types of intelligence sources available, including internal data repositories, open sources, commercial sources, and industry organizations. They will learn how to assess each source's confidence and reliability and determine which are best suited to support their intelligence requirements.

- Example: An organization operating in the healthcare industry may find that commercial sources, such as threat intelligence portals and services, offer targeted and curated intelligence products relevant to their sector.

- **Establish Collection Objectives and Capabilities:** Participants will learn to determine the specific data sources and collection plans required to support their intelligence requirements. They will understand how to cross-reference and validate data from multiple sources to provide additional situational context and improve the accuracy of their CTI products.
  - Example: An organization focused on identifying and mitigating threats to its critical infrastructure may prioritize collecting information related to industrial control systems (ICS) and using tools that can detect and prevent ICS-specific threats.

- **Determine Intelligence Tooling Dependencies:** Participants will learn how to determine the technical dependencies required to support their CTI tools and understand how they can integrate with other security tools and data sources. They will also be able to estimate the costs associated with intelligence tooling subscriptions and other dependencies.
  - Example: organizations that relies on commercial sources may need to factor in the cost of subscriptions to these services when building its program budget.

It is also essential to consider the costs associated with intelligence tooling subscriptions and dependencies. This involves evaluating the prices of different tools and their respective capabilities and limitations. It is important to carefully consider the costs of these tools and the long-term benefits they will provide to the organization to make informed decisions about the resources that will be invested in the CTI program.

The end goal of any CTI program is to defend against emerging cyber threats and keep systems secure effectively. By taking the time to identify and evaluate intelligence sources, determine collection objectives and capabilities, and understand the value of these sources, participants will be well on their way to building a robust CTI program that supports their organization's operational security.

Intelligence Sources

Building a comprehensive CTI program requires careful planning, effective collection strategies, and access to various intelligence sources. These sources can come from internal and external sources and include free and paid options.

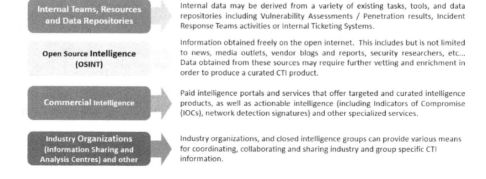

Internal Teams, Resources and Data Repositories — Internal data may be derived from a variety of existing tasks, tools, and data repositories including Vulnerability Assessments / Penetration results, Incident Response Teams activities or Internal Ticketing Systems.

Open Source Intelligence (OSINT) — Information obtained freely on the open internet. This includes but is not limited to news, media outlets, vendor blogs and reports, security researchers, etc... Data obtained from these sources may require further vetting and enrichment in order to produce a curated CTI product.

Commercial Intelligence — Paid intelligence portals and services that offer targeted and curated intelligence products, as well as actionable intelligence (including Indicators of Compromise (IOCs), network detection signatures) and other specialized services.

Industry Organizations (Information Sharing and Analysis Centres) and other — Industry organizations, and closed intelligence groups can provide various means for coordinating, collaborating and sharing industry and group specific CTI information.

Internal teams and data repositories are key internal sources of CTI information. This information can be gathered from various activities, including vulnerability assessments, penetration testing results, incident response activities, and internal ticketing systems. These sources provide a wealth of data that can be processed and analyzed to provide relevant intelligence information. For example, analyzing data from internal incident response activities can give organizations insight into the nature and source of cyber threats, allowing them to take appropriate measures to defend.

Open-source intelligence data (OSINT) is another vital source of CTI information. This data is freely available on the open internet and includes news and media outlets, vendor blogs, security research publications, and others. OSINT sources should be vetted and enriched to provide relevant and actionable intelligence. For example, monitoring news articles about a specific type of malware can give organizations early warning of potential threats and help them take preventative measures.

Commercial intelligence is another source of CTI information. This type of intelligence is available through paid intelligence portals and services, which offer targeted and curated intelligence products, as well as actionable intelligence in the form of Indicators of Compromise (IOCs), network detection signatures, and others. Subscribing to a commercial intelligence service that provides alerts on the latest cyber threats can help organizations stay ahead of the threat landscape and respond quickly to emerging threats.

Industry organizations, such as Information Sharing and Analysis Centers (ISACs), are closed intelligence groups that provide members with the ability to coordinate, collaborate, and share industry-specific CTI information. Joining an industry ISAC can provide organizations with access to relevant and timely information on emerging cyber threats specific to their industry. For example, a financial services ISAC can provide banks and financial institutions with the intelligence they need to defend against cyber threats targeting their industry.

It's important to remember that all sources of CTI must be vetted, reviewed, and categorized to ensure their confidence and reliability. The quality of the intelligence you receive is only as good as the quality of the sources you use. By incorporating various internal and external sources into your CTI program, you can build a comprehensive picture of the cyber threat landscape and take action to defend against emerging threats.

Internal Sources

Internal sources are an essential component of a Cyber Threat Intelligence program as they provide unique and valuable information specific to the organization. By leveraging internal data, organizations can gain insights into potential threats that would not be available from external sources. For example, internal device logs can reveal patterns of suspicious activity, while business data can inform decisions related to risk management and security investments.

Internal sources can also complement external data collection efforts, filling in gaps and providing a more comprehensive understanding of the threat landscape. Utilizing internal sources can also ensure that intelligence products and services are of the highest quality, as the information is directly relevant to the organization's specific needs.

Examples of this include but are not limited to:

- **Business intelligence reporting**: This includes data and reports on various aspects of the organization, such as customer behavior, financial performance, and operational efficiency. This information can help to identify potential security threats, such as insider threats and unauthorized access to sensitive information.

- **Device, Network, and application logs:** This data can provide detailed information on the organization's usage of devices and applications. For example, device logs can reveal patterns of suspicious activity, while application logs can help to track the use of specific applications and identify potential security risks.

- **Security Tools:** This includes but is not limited to network vulnerability scanners, End-Point detection and Response Tools (EDR), and Intrusion Detection /Intrusion Prevention (IDS/IPS) Tools. This information provides clear visibility into the security threats and activities that your organization is facing.

By analyzing internal data, organizations can better understand potential threats, inform decision-making, and improve the accuracy and quality of their intelligence products and services. This can lead to a complete understanding of the organization's security posture, better-targeted mitigation strategies, and an overall improvement in network security.

Open-Source Data (OSINT)

OSINT refers to information that is publicly available and easily accessible from various sources, including websites, online databases, research sites, blogs, forums, news outlets, and more. However, it's crucial to be cautious when collecting and using OSINT data, as not all sources may be trustworthy or unbiased.

It's essential to validate the sources and cross-reference the information with other reputable sources to ensure the accuracy and reliability of the data collected for CTI. Several methods for collecting OSINT data exist, such as manual collection, automatic downloading, and scraping using custom-built tools. Additionally, there are online services that offer API access and integrations, which can speed up data collection and enrichment. The more automation and API services you have enabled, the more effective your data collection processes will be.

To guarantee the reliability of the information collected, it's imperative to only use authoritative and reputable sources and to review and update them regularly. The sources used may change over time, so it's crucial to keep them up to date to ensure the most accurate and relevant data is used in your CTI program.

OSINT is a valuable source of information for CTI and should be used with care and caution. Organizations should focus on using only authoritative and reliable sources, prioritize quality over quantity, and regularly review and update their sources to ensure their CTI program remains operationalized and relevant to their needs. By following best practices and being mindful of potential pitfalls, organizations can effectively leverage the information from OSINT and improve their overall cyber security posture.

Social Media (SOCMINT)

SOCMINT is a valuable source of information that can assist organizations in profiling individuals of interest. By identifying connections, accomplices, events, timelines, and other profile details, SOCMINT can support threat actor tracking and profiling initiatives. Additionally, SOCMINT can be used to identify scammers promoting fake products and monitor mentions of emerging threats. It can also provide insight into public comments indicating malicious intent by potential threat actors on forums, chat rooms, and social media platforms.

Twitter is a handy platform for SOCMINT, as it allows organizations to monitor real-time events, comments, and conversation threads of those they are following. By leveraging the quality of Twitter profiles, organizations can be alerted in near-real times of emerging cyber threats as these threats arise and circulate through the platform. Security researchers can also use social media to investigate and share information about emerging threats. This information can be helpful for organizations to implement proactive controls to defend against newly identified threats. The researchers can confirm or deny threats by analyzing the data and sharing additional information they have discovered.

SOCMINT is an essential aspect of CTI that organizations should pay attention to. By leveraging the vast amounts of data available on social media platforms, organizations can stay ahead of emerging threats and reduce the risk of being caught off guard by a cyber-attack. To effectively collect and analyze this information, organizations should develop a comprehensive SOCMINT collection plan that outlines the sources to be monitored, the information to be collected, and the methodology to be used.

Commercial Sources

Commercial vendors specialize in specific areas of intelligence, such as Indicator of Compromise (IOC) feeds, data enrichment, and research tools. They may provide platforms for investigations and research as well as API integration with other security tools, allowing for real-time data exchange and updates. This enables organizations to quickly access the latest intelligence and integrate it into their existing security systems. Commercial vendors may also offer high-confidence data and data enrichment capabilities, which may not be accessible in-house. They may have custom tools or access to additional data sources to enhance intelligence gathering and analysis. This can be a more cost-effective option than building and maintaining similar devices internally.

When considering commercial sources for intelligence gathering, it's essential to assess the maturity of the CTI program and determine if utilizing commercial vendors is a priority in the short or long term. While commercial services can be expensive and require dedicated human resources, they can provide a better return on investment (ROI) than other security controls or tools. Each commercial threat intelligence vendor has a unique niche in the marketplace, offering specific data types. They can expedite the production of intelligence products and provide high-confidence data and research tools that may not be accessible in-house.

Utilizing commercial sources in a CTI program can offer valuable support, expertise, and access to intelligence that may only be available in some places. It's essential to use metrics to assess the effectiveness of intelligence gathering and make informed decisions about the resources allocated to the CTI program.

Dark Web

The Dark Web (also called the Deep Web) is a hidden part of the internet that is not accessible through traditional search engines and requires specialized software that provides a platform for anonymous and encrypted communication, making it a popular destination for cyber criminals and other malicious actors.

The Dark Web provides valuable intelligence for CTI teams, as it can provide information on new and emerging threats and details about cybercriminals' tactics, techniques, and procedures (TTPs). This information can be collected from various sources such as Dark Web forums, marketplaces, and chat rooms, commonly used by cyber criminals to discuss, buy and sell illegal goods and services and communicate with each other.

Some commercial vendors specialize in Dark Web intelligence and can also play a role in providing valuable insights into underground marketplaces and forums where malicious actors may buy, sell, and share information relevant to an organization. These vendors can also offer translation services, as much of the content on the Dark Web is in foreign languages, and conduct Requests for Information (RFIs) based on an organization's priority intelligence requirements.

Some examples of Dark Web intelligence sources include:

- **Dark Web forums:** Cybercriminals often use forums on the Dark Web to discuss and share information about their activities, including new exploits, malware, and tools. CTI teams can monitor these forums to gather intelligence on potential threats.

- **Dark Web marketplaces:** Cybercriminals often buy and sell illegal goods and services on the Dark Web, including stolen data, malware, and hacking tools. CTI teams can monitor these marketplaces to gather intelligence on the latest offerings and trends.

- **Dark Web chat rooms:** Cybercriminals often use chat rooms on the Dark Web to communicate and coordinate their activities. CTI teams can monitor these chat rooms to gather intelligence on the latest threats and the groups behind them.

It is strongly suggested that Dark Web activities are not performed internally.

- The deep dark web is not indexed, and you must know the Onion URL to find the website / marketplace / forum you wish. (i.e. http://juhanurmihxlp77nkq76byazcldy2hlmovfu2epvl5ankdibsot4csyd[.]onion)
- Illicit forums and marketplace do not take kindly to newcomers. Even if you found an appropriate marketplace, you must register/apply and go through a vetting process. If you enter the marketplace, you will not have any reputation, and most members will not speak with you.
- These forums and marketplaces are filled with sophisticated hackers and other criminals – if they have a reason or suspect you are up to something, it is unknown what they may do.
- These are international marketplaces where people of all languages participate unless you have employees who can translate forum threads. You otherwise won't be able to make sense of the threads.
- Security concerns, as you are going to illicit websites that could be used to deliver malicious code to your computer with some virus.
- OPSEC (i.e., VPNs) do not always ensure 100% privacy,
- Internal legal teams typically have concerns as the DDW is commonly a grey area primarily believed to be associated with illegal activity.
- It requires significant effort and resources to monitor effectively.

If you are just starting to build your threat intelligence program, dark web monitoring should not be a requirement.

It is recommended to include dark web monitoring after your program has been established, is a fairly mature operation, and has enough Intelligence Requirements to support a vendor.

Metrics would be required to determine and track the effectiveness of the Dark Web to detect controls and other means to mitigate risk.

For the price of a dark web vendor this budget may be better off on other security controls and tools, that may provide a better ROI.

Please consult your legal counsel before exploring the option of using the Dark Web.

The Dark Web is a valuable intelligence source for CTI teams, and leveraging this information can enable organizations to proactively defend against potential threats and respond quickly and effectively to actual incidents. It is recommended that organizations avoid conducting Dark Web activities in-house, as accessing the deep Dark Web requires specialized software and knowledge of the relevant onion URL. Engaging with a vendor specializing in Dark Web intelligence can provide organizations with the necessary expertise and resources to effectively gather intelligence from this hidden part of the internet.

Trusted Community Sources and Industry Organizations Information Sharing and Analysis Centers (ISACs)

One valuable source of information is targeted communities, such as Industry-Specific Information Sharing and Analysis Centers (ISACs) and Circles of Trust. These communities bring together individuals and organizations who are committed to sharing intelligence and insights specifically related to their industries or relationships. By participating in these communities, you can gain valuable insights into sector-specific cyber threats, as well as information about upcoming conferences and services. This can help you stay ahead of the curve and protect your organization from potential threats.

Below are examples of various communities:

- **Information Sharing and Analysis Centers:** FS-ISAC (Financial Services Information Sharing and Analysis Center) is a community of financial services organizations that share intelligence on cyber threats specific to their industry. Many other sectors have ISACs, such as Retail, Electricity, health care, etc.....)

- **Circle of Trust**: a small group of organizations within a particular sector that agree to share information. For instance, five banks within Canada might establish an information-sharing agreement to collaborate on defending the Canadian financial services sector.

- **Trusted security research groups:** Slack channels, mailing lists, and Discord groups are communities of security researchers who come together to share information on cyber threats. These groups can be free to join, but there is often no vetting process, and threat actors may infiltrate the group to gain information or spread disinformation.

Joining a community or ISAC may require an annual membership fee ranging from a few thousand to tens of thousands of dollars. The membership cost can increase oversight and security, reducing the risk of infiltration by threat actors. It is essential to carefully consider the price and level of security each community or ISAC provides and the sector-specific or relationship-specific intelligence they provide when building a CTI program. Trusted communities and ISACs can be valuable sources of information for defending against cyber threats.

In addition to ISACs, other trusted communities, such as Circles of Trust, are groups of select organizations that agree to share information. There are also trusted security research groups, such as slack channels, mailing lists, or discord groups, where security researchers come together to share information and discuss threats. The level of security and cost associated with these communities can vary greatly. Some communities, like slack or Discord communities, may not have a vetting process and may have threat actors infiltrating them. On the other hand, Circles of Trust have agreements, contracts, and higher oversight to ensure that only the appropriate people are involved in discussions.

Choosing the right communities or ISACs is an important decision for protecting an organization's assets and information. Factors such as cost, security level, and type of information shared must be evaluated before deciding. Participating in trusted communities and ISACs can provide valuable resources and insights for defending against cyber threats and mitigating risks.

Collection Plans

Collection Plans are an essential component of a Cyber Threat Intelligence (CTI) program. The collection plan outlines the sources that will be leveraged to obtain the relevant information required for the CTI program and how this will be achieved.

Collection Plans should answer the following questions:
- What sources will be consulted (internal sources, open sources, commercial tools, etc.) to obtain the necessary information?
- How will the information be collected (i.e. automated alerts, manual efforts, RSS Feeds, Push notification, custom scripts)?
- What are the objectives of the intelligence requirements?

Intelligence Requirements (IRs):
• Identify emerging threats/exploited vulnerabilities
• Determine if the organization is exposed to these threats, and identify exposed systems
• Determine detection/protection measures required to defend against these threats and provide these to the necessary teams.
• Raise awareness to stakeholders regarding the situation.

Collection Plans:	
Internal:	• Leverage vulnerability scanning tools such as Tenable to perform scanning to identify potentially vulnerable.
Open Source:	• Monitor media sources and technology related websites to identify emerging exploitation of Zero-day and Critical vulnerabilities. • Monitor Vendor sites for related security advisories and patch/mitigation efforts.
Social Media:	• N/A
Commercial:	• N/A

To monitor emerging threats, data collection sources could include security vendors, research blogs, and information security communities. In addition, internal sources that can be leveraged include vulnerability scanning tools, such as Tenable, to identify potential vulnerabilities. For open-source information, the collection plan could consist of monitoring media sources, technology-related websites, and vendor sites for security advisories, identifying Indicators of Compromise (IOCs), and detection rules to defend against the exploitation of vulnerabilities.

To validate findings, it is recommended to use multiple sources and other means of enrichment. Collection sources should be mapped to intelligence requirements and rated based on the NATO system and the Admiralty Code. This system provides a ranking and rating of the reliability and confidence of the information source. For example, the reliability scale ranges from completely reliable (A) to completely unreliable (F). In contrast, the credibility scale ranges from confirmed by multiple independent sources (1) to the truth that cannot be judged (6). When evaluating sources, a score is given for both reliability and credibility. A score of D4, for example, would indicate that the information could be more reliable but has provided valid data in the past.

The frequency with that collection tasks must be performed also needs to be established. This can range from ad-hoc activities to daily or hourly checks through automation. The frequency will depend on the severity and importance of the intelligence requirement. For example, a weekly review may be sufficient if the intelligence requirement is low frequency or severity. On the other hand, if you're using social media data sources, it's best to have a social media sock puppet account to cover your IP address and logs. This helps ensure that operational security requirements are met.

Additionally, you may need dedicated intelligence systems or infrastructure, such as a lab environment, to leverage information and access specific sensitive sources. For example, dirty lines (separate internet connections from the corporate internet) can create segregation between your environment and the internal corporate network. This helps ensure that if an IP address is exposed, it does not impact the corporate environment. To further ensure security, it's best to use a different internet service provider for your lab environment than the one used for your corporate environment. For example, using Bell Internet for the corporate environment and Rogers Internet for the lab environment provides segregation between the service providers, ensuring no correlation between the two.

A collection plan for a Cyber Threat Intelligence (CTI) program is crucial for ensuring the operational security of systems. When building the collection plan, consider the following key points:
- Identify the right intelligence sources.
- Establish clear collection objectives and capabilities.
- Determine the value of the intelligence collected.
- Consider cost factors.

Keeping these considerations in mind will help ensure that the collection plan effectively supports the operational security of systems.

Action items

It is important to establish a comprehensive collection plan for intelligence requirements. This plan should include the sources of intelligence to be used and the objectives to be achieved. When selecting the sources, it is important to consider the credibility and reliability of the site and producer, prioritize the sources based on the type of information they can provide, and continually monitor and adjust the plan as needed. This will ensure a systematic and effective intelligence collection plan is developed to meet the established requirements.

For each intelligence requirements determine your collection plans and data sources for:

Internal Sources:
- Determine if any internal data sources (business applications, team members, or business unit outputs and reports) could be of value based on your intelligence requirements.
- Business Applications
- Application logs
- Helpdesk tickets submitted by employees (i.e., ServiceNow, Jira)

Internal Teams:
- Security:
- What type of incidents does your security team see most?

- Vulnerability management:
- What vulnerabilities are still exposed within your environment?

Social Media:
- Depending on the intelligence requirement for social media sources, determine if there is a need to create social media accounts on various platforms or if data can be publicly viewed.
- Determine which platforms are in scope, and if a social media account registration is required, ensure you use a sock puppet-type account to ensure the anonymity of you and your organization.
- Disable options that may allow for data leakage (i.e., how you appear to someone when you view their profile.)
- Follow the Social Media accounts of:
  o Associated vendor and competitor.
  o Cyber Security Influencers associated with your industry.
  o Cyber Security researchers and organizations.
- Identify hashtags and keywords associated with your industry or organization.

Commercial Sources:
- Ensure your intelligence requirements are clearly defined, and determine which vendors provide intelligence services that meet your requirements.
- Determine how you are going to action the findings.
- What internal tools (intelligence or security) could integrate with the vendor, and what would that do?
- Determine if existing tools provide integrations with commercial services and if they are already in production.

- Contact commercial vendors and get into their sales cycle, get the demo, share the PIRs, request a trial period, and evaluate multiple products (Always ensure non-disclosure agreements are in place).
- Be creative and customize the services as required.

Trusted communities and ISACs:
- Determine what specific role a trusted community or ISAC would play within your threat intelligence program.
- If budgeting permits, joining and participating in the appropriate ISAC is recommended. You will interact with other members of the community and be able to share business experiences, pain points, vendor experiences, as well as threat-related information. In addition, ISACs frequently have private forums, events, and presentations which can also be leveraged for your internal intelligence program.
- If budgeting is a constraint, there are alternatives to ISAC, such as trusted communities found in Slack / Discord Groups or other newsgroups.
- For most new intelligence programs, communities and ISACs are not necessarily required, but if you have funding and capabilities, it would be an asset.

Other Action Items:
- Take note of dependencies within each requirement.
- Evaluate credibility of sources, accuracy of information provided as well as the reliability of the data.
- Understand costs associated with tools, platforms, and data.
- Identify how to consume and produce data and other intelligence products.
- Consider special tools, integrations, custom scripts or open-source tools, and other technical requirements.

- Understand the cost of each intelligence required to support the business case for pursuing the requirement.
- Prioritize intelligence requirements by cost-benefit analysis.

Summary

In this chapter, we focused on understanding the crucial role of intelligence sources and collection plans in building a Cyber Threat Intelligence (CTI) program. The aim was to equip participants with the necessary knowledge to identify and evaluate suitable sources, platforms, and tools to support their intelligence requirements and to establish clear collection objectives and capabilities. It is crucial to understand that not all intelligence sources are created equal. Participants learned how to assess the value of intelligence sources and how they can support their overall CTI program. They also learned about the cost factors associated with intelligence tooling subscriptions and other dependencies required to support each intelligence requirement.

The next chapter will dive into the various products that can be produced and distributed as part of a comprehensive Cyber Threat Intelligence (CTI) program. The aim is to help participants understand the different formats in which CTI products can be delivered to stakeholders and how each product can assist in defending against emerging cyber threats. Participants will learn about the various formats in which these products can be provided and how they can be utilized to defend against emerging cyber threats. The goal is to equip participants with the necessary knowledge to effectively distribute CTI products to stakeholders and help defend against cyber-attacks.

Chapter #4c – IR - Courses-of-Action, Service Catalogue, Communication Plans, and Services Level Agreements (SLAs)

Introduction

This chapter is part of a more extensive methodology that focuses on the activities and outputs of the Cyber Threat Intelligence (CTI) team. The goal of the CTI team is to respond to alerts raised as intelligence requirements and implement controls to mitigate risk or communicate findings to relevant teams and stakeholders. This is achieved by producing CTI products, services, and other activities aligned with established Service Level Agreements (SLAs) and delivered promptly.

Intelligence requirements	• Leverage discovery information to determine what threats scenarios in scope. • Identify applicable sources for intelligence data. • Determine products and services the CTI team can produce to mitigate cyber threats and reduce risk. • Establish Communication Plans and SLAs
Intelligence tools	• Determine tools to collect, store, & process data. • Understand how various intelligence tools can integrate with each other as well as other security tools, or data sources. • Determine technical dependencies to support CTI tools.

In the next chapter, the focus will be more on intelligence tools needed to collect, store, and process data and understand how these tools can integrate with other security tools and data sources. The team will also determine the technical dependencies required to support CTI tools. The goal is to comprehensively understand the intelligence tools used by the CTI team and how they work together to support the overall goal of reducing cyber threats and managing risk.

Chapter Objectives

This chapter is designed to help participants to establish a robust CTI program. These skills will aid participants in developing key elements of a CTI program, such as:

- **Courses-of-Action (COAs):** Participants will learn how to identify and categorize COAs, and actions taken by the CTI team to defend against emerging cyber threats. They will also understand how to measure the effectiveness and maturity of these COAs in defending against cyber threats.

- **Service Catalogue:** Participants will learn how to design a comprehensive list of intelligence services and products the CTI team offers. This will provide stakeholders with a clear understanding of the services and products available to them.

- **Communication Plans:** Participants will learn how to develop communication plans for each product or service offered by the CTI team, specifying the intended recipients and the mode of communication (e.g., email, pdf report).

- **Services Level Agreements (SLAs):** Participants will be able to implement SLAs, which are agreements that outline the standards of service expected by the stakeholders. This will help ensure that the services the CTI team provides meet the stakeholders' expectations.

By mastering these skills, participants will be able to design, implement, and maintain a CTI program that effectively protects against cyber threats and supports the organization's security objectives.

Courses-of-Action (COAs)

As a cyber security professional, I would like to emphasize that Courses of Action (COAs) play a crucial role in a Cyber Threat Intelligence (CTI) program. They provide a structured and effective method for the CTI team to respond to emerging cyber threats, mitigating associated risks and enhancing the organization's security posture.

COAs define the specific actions the CTI analyst will take when a threat is detected. The type and complexity of COAs implemented will depend on the maturity level and capabilities of the organization's security tools and infrastructure. For organizations with advanced security tools, sophisticated COAs can be implemented, such as blocking malicious domains, hunting for potential threats, and implementing detection and prevention signatures based on emerging threats. On the other hand, organizations with limited resources may need to implement more basic COAs, such as sending an email to raise awareness.

It is important for the CTI team to have a clear understanding of the available resources and capabilities, including what may need to be obtained from vendors, to make informed decisions about the COAs to implement. This will help ensure that the CTI team's actions align with the organization's security objectives and goals.

It's important to note that when recommending COAs that need to be performed by other teams, it's best to consult with the Subject Matter Experts (SMEs) to determine if the recommendation would impact existing controls. SMEs are the experts in their respective fields and should make the final decision on whether to implement the recommendations and assess any potential operational or security impacts.

Classification

The classification of Courses of Action (COAs) within a Cyber Threat Intelligence (CTI) program organizes the various responses and actions the CTI team can take when dealing with emerging threats. By categorizing COAs, the CTI team can better understand their strengths and weaknesses in defending against these threats and use this information to identify areas for improvement and prioritize future investments in security capabilities.

Courses-of-Actions fall into four main classifications:

Strategic	• Executive level awareness, reporting, and guidance.
Operational	• Enhancements to internal processes, procedures and detection capabilities.
Tactical	• provides info related to TTPs used by threat actors (attackers) to perform attacks
Technical	• provides information about an attacker's resources that are used to perform the attack.

- They are also known as classifications of products and services the CTI team produces.
- Depending on your intelligence products and capabilities, your courses of action may be focused on one or many of these areas.
- This is fine if your products, recommendations, and efforts effectively mitigate or reduce risk.

A Cyber Threat Intelligence (CTI) program focuses on courses of action (COAs) to mitigate or reduce risk to an organization. It is important to ensure that the selected COAs are effective and to classify and prioritize them to continually improve defense against emerging cyber threats. By doing so, the CTI team can make informed decisions, allocate resources effectively, and track progress over time to stay ahead of the evolving threat landscape.

Categorization

Categorizing Courses-of-Action (COAs) in a Cyber Threat Intelligence (CTI) program is crucial for evaluating an organization's ability to defend against threats and improving response effectiveness. By categorizing COAs, the CTI team can quickly determine the best course of action, minimize damage to the organization, and continuously improve response procedures to handle future threats. Categorizing COAs is a key component in developing a comprehensive CTI program.

The seven categories that COAs typically fall into are: discover, detect, deny, disrupt, degrade, deceive, and destroy.

| Discover | • Historical searches in the environment to see if indicators have been seen before |

| Detect | • Future monitoring of indicators (invest into SIEM) - Triggers alters |

| Deny | • Prevent or block event from occurring |

| Disrupt | • Interferes with threat actors actions |

| Degrade | • Slows down threat actors capability |

| Deceive | • Leads threat actor to believe the intended event was successful (sink-holing) |

| Destroy | • Offensive actions taken to reduce an adversaries capacity for future intrusion (hacking back / DDoS) |

- **Discover** is the historical search within the environment to see if indicators of compromise (IOCs) have been seen before. This involves hunting the environment with specific IOCs obtained from various threat sources to find any signs of historical compromise or infection.

- **Detect** refers to future monitoring of indicators, such as ingesting them into a Security Information and Event Management (SIEM) system to trigger alerts on future infections or detections of malicious activity.

- **Deny** refers to preventative actions or blocking events from occurring outright. This may involve firewalls, intrusion prevention systems, or other security measures to stop malicious activity.

- **Disrupt** refers to actions that interfere with the threat actors' activities, such as disrupting the communication between malware and its command-and-control center.

- **Degrade** refers to actions taken to slow down a threat actor's capability to perform malicious activity, such as slowing down their movement through the network.

- **Deceive** refers to actions that mislead the threat actor into thinking that their intended events were successful, such as sending them to a sinkhole where the traffic goes nowhere.

- **Destroy** refers to offensive actions that reduce an adversary's capacity for future intrusion. This category includes hacking back and distributed denial of service (DDoS) attacks, but it is essential to be cautious about these actions as there may be legal implications.

Categorizing Courses of Action (COAs) in a Cyber Threat Intelligence (CTI) program is critical for ensuring effective responses to cyber threats. COA categorization provides a framework for evaluating response options based on the nature of the threat, available resources, and the organization's goals. This categorization streamlines decision-making, ensures consistent responses, fosters collaboration, and helps measure the success of actions taken.

Service Catalogue

Incorporating COAs into a CTI Service Catalogue helps organizations to provide comprehensive and actionable intelligence to stakeholders in a structured and consistent manner. A CTI Service Catalogue is a list of intelligence services and products the CTI team provides. It includes detailed descriptions of the services offered, including each service's purpose, scope, and objectives.

As discussed in previous sections, the first step in building a CTI program is to define the intelligence requirements. The next s to determine the COAs that need to be taken for each intelligence requirement. Finally, these intelligence requirements and COAs are grouped into a product or service the CTI team offers.

Each product or service may comprise smaller products or services, each with its unique format and recipient. For example, the CTI team may work closely with the security operations team to create Indicator of Compromise (IOC) feeds, automatically ingested into a security information and event management (SIEM) system. At the same time, threat detection signatures may be provided by email to a security engineer, and threat landscape reporting may be delivered to security management or directors in the form of PowerPoint presentations.

This approach allows the CTI team to tailor the intelligence services and products to ensure alignment with their overall security objectives, ensuring information is delivered in a format that is easy to understand and use. By grouping the COAs into products and services, the CTI team can also measure the effectiveness of their services and continuously improve the quality and value of their offerings.

Incorporating Cyber Threat Intelligence (CTI) into a Service Catalogue helps organizations to standardize and align their CTI services with their security goals, prioritize efforts and resources, and improve the quality and value of the services. The Service Catalogue acts as a centralized repository for information on CTI services and provides a clear framework for delivering these services consistently and reliably.

Security Operations Centre (SOC) Services

CTI plays a vital role in supporting the Security Operations Center (SOC) by providing a deeper and more comprehensive understanding of the cyber threats that an organization faces. The critical information obtained from CTI enables the development of Courses of Action (COAs), which outline the steps the CTI team will take in response to a detected threat. These COAs can range from basic awareness-raising activities to complex control implementations, depending on the resources and capabilities available.

Implementing these COAs can support the SOC's monitoring and operations by providing a structured and practical approach to responding to emerging threats. For instance, COAs may include blocking known malicious domains, implementing detection and prevention signatures based on emerging threats, or engaging in threat-hunting activities to proactively identify potential threats.

The CTI team plays a crucial role in supporting the SOC by providing an in-depth understanding of an organization's cyber threats. The CTI team can use Courses of Action (COAs) to respond to threats in a structured and effective manner and to facilitate communication and collaboration with the SOC. COAs may include reporting threat actor infrastructure for the takedown, sending awareness emails to relevant parties, blocking malicious domains, and implementing detection and prevention signatures. By using COAs, the CTI team can support the SOC's efforts and enhance the overall security posture of the organization.

Incident Response Services

The purpose of a Cyber Threat Intelligence (CTI) team is to provide crucial information and support to the Incident Response (IR) team during a security breach. The CTI team is responsible for providing the IR team with relevant and up-to-date threat intelligence to aid in their investigation and enable them to comprehend the nature and extent of a security breach. This information may encompass information about prevalent attack methods, techniques, and tactics employed by malicious actors, as well as details about well-known malware and other threats.

One of the ways in which CTI teams can offer support to IR teams is by detecting Indicators of Compromise (IOCs) linked to a security breach. IOCs may consist of malicious IP addresses, domains, hashes, and file names that can be used to identify and monitor malicious activity. The CTI team's proficiency in analyzing malicious activity can be highly valuable in assisting IR teams to promptly recognize and track the source and progression of a security breach.

CTI teams can also support IR teams by attributing an attack to a specific threat actor or group. This involves analyzing the tactics, techniques, and procedures (TTPs) utilized in the attack, as well as information about the attacker's past activities and infrastructure. Attributing an attack can provide IR teams with valuable insight into the motivations and goals of the attacker, which can aid in developing efficient mitigation and remediation strategies.

Moreover, CTI teams can work in tandem with IR teams to ensure a coordinated and effective response to security incidents. This collaboration involves sharing information and intelligence and jointly creating and implementing mitigation and remediation strategies. CTI teams are well-versed in tracking threat actors and analyzing malicious activity, making their expertise invaluable in devising effective strategies for responding to security incidents. By utilizing the CTI team's resources, organizations can effectively manage security incidents, minimize the impact of attacks, and strengthen their overall security posture.

Vulnerability Management (Examples)

Vulnerability Management is a critical component of an organization's overall cybersecurity strategy. It involves the identification, evaluation, and prioritization of vulnerabilities in an organization's systems and networks and the development of a plan to mitigate or eliminate those vulnerabilities. Vulnerability Management is important because vulnerabilities can be exploited by cybercriminals to gain unauthorized access to an organization's systems and data, causing significant damage and harm.

This is where CTI can help support. By providing actionable intelligence about emerging threats. This information enables organizations to prioritize their work and focus on the most critical vulnerabilities first. CTI can also provide recommendations for mitigating or preventing the exploitation of vulnerabilities, such as implementing specific security controls to help the Vulnerability Management team make informed decisions. This coordination between the CTI and Vulnerability Management teams builds synergy and helps to ensure that the organization responds to threats comprehensively and effectively. By working together, these teams can reduce the risk of cyber threats and support the organization's overall security objectives.

The CTI team can also provide guidance on how to mitigate or prevent the exploitation of vulnerabilities. For example, CTI can recommend implementing specific security controls, such as firewalls, intrusion detection systems, or access control systems, to prevent the exploitation of the vulnerability. This helps the Vulnerability Management and network security teams to make informed decisions about the most effective ways to address the vulnerability.

CTI can provide a wealth of information to support Vulnerability Management. Examples of the types of actionable content CTI can include technical reports on actively exploited vulnerabilities, strategic advisories on the threat landscape, monitoring and identification of updates and security patches, and recommendations for determining risk and exposure based on threat details. All these support Vulnerability Management's mission to protect the organization from cyber threats.

In conclusion, CTI plays a crucial role in supporting Vulnerability Management. By providing valuable insights into emerging threats and their potential impact, CTI helps organizations prioritize their work, respond to threats comprehensively and effectively, and reduce the risk of cyber-attacks. CTI is an important component of a comprehensive cybersecurity strategy and is essential for organizations that want to stay ahead of emerging threats and defend themselves against cyber-attacks.

Awareness and Reporting

The CTI team is the backbone of this program and plays a crucial role in ensuring the security of the organization. Their responsibility is to gather, analyze, and disseminate threat intelligence information that is essential for organizations to comprehend the current threat landscape and the potential risks and vulnerabilities that need to be addressed. This information is used by the CTI team to inform the development of Courses of Action (COAs) and to strengthen the overall security posture of the organization.

Regular awareness and reporting can be delivered through various channels, depending on the intended audience and the format of the report. For instance, while regular email updates may be sufficient for non-technical stakeholders, technical teams and management may require more in-depth reports and presentations. It is important to carefully consider the reporting format and intended audience when selecting the appropriate delivery mechanism. For example, regular email updates may be sufficient for non-technical stakeholders, but technical teams and management may require more in-depth reports and presentations. This ensures that everyone has access to the information they need to understand the current threat landscape and take appropriate action to enhance the organization's security posture.

The benefit of CTI regular awareness and reporting is twofold. Firstly, it helps to build a culture of security within the organization by keeping all stakeholders informed and engaged in enhancing the organization's security posture. This helps to ensure that everyone is aware of the latest threats and measures to address them. Secondly, it enables organizations to stay ahead of emerging threats by providing the necessary information to address potential vulnerabilities proactively.

A comprehensive CTI program that includes regular awareness and reporting is essential for organizations to maintain their security posture and reduce the risk of cyber threats. By providing regular updates and reports, the CTI team helps organizations stay informed, engaged, and proactive, which ultimately enhances their security posture and reduces the risk of cyber threats.

Daily Threat Reporting Services

CTI Daily Reports provide organizations with a consistent and up-to-date view of the current threat landscape. This information is critical for organizations to prioritize their security efforts and allocate resources effectively. By staying informed about the latest threats and trends, organizations can be better prepared to defend against them and maintain a proactive posture regarding cybersecurity.

These reports can be customized to meet an organization's specific needs. For example, an organization that is at high risk of targeted attacks may focus more on threat actor activity, while another organization with a mature security posture may prioritize the technical analysis of specific threats. This customization ensures that the information in the reports is relevant and actionable for the organization.

Daily Threat Intelligence Brief – March 13ᵗʰ, 2019

Analyst: Robert Vidal

Wednesday March 13ᵗʰ, 2019

Third-Party Online Chat Service Responsible for Data Breach Affecting Best Buy, Delta Airlines and Sears Holdings

Severity: HIGH

Attack Vector: Supply Chain Attack

Details:

- The breach occurred between September 26ᵗʰ, and October 12ᵗʰ, of 2017, when malware infected the systems of [24]7.ai, an online chat service.
- It is believed the threat actor gained access to payment card numbers, CVVs, and expiration dates, as well as names and addresses of those compromised. A Delta spokesperson stated that less than 100,000 customers were affected, yet hundreds of thousands more could potentially be exposed.
- The malware was removed on October 12ᵗʰ, 2017 and [24]7.ai spent five and a half months investigating the incident together with law enforcement.

Risk and Impact: With this information it is possible for threat actors to use the compromised data for financial fraud against the victims.

Recommendations: It is recommended that organizations have processes and procedures in place to assess security risks and concerns related to the integration of third party tools used within public facing applications. In addition, Incident Handling Procedures should be in place and ready in the event of an incident to prevent prolonged investigations.

Associated CVEs: 2018-2385

Courses of Action:

- Vulnerability Management notified of the vulnerable CVE and advised the associated patch was applied during the previous patch cycle.
- IOCs obtained and searched within the SIEM with no detections discovered.
- IOCs added to ongoing monitoring.

References: Bleeping Computers

The content of CTI Daily Reports will vary depending on the organization's specific requirements and objectives, but may include information such as:

Emerging threats: A summary of the latest threats and trends, including malware, phishing attacks, and other cyber threats.

Vulnerabilities: A summary of the latest vulnerabilities, including those newly discovered or patched.

Indicators of Compromise (IoCs): Details of specific threats, including indicators of compromise such as IP addresses, domains, and file hashes.

Recommended actions: Recommendations for mitigating the threat, including best practices and remediation steps.

The target audience for CTI Daily Reports may include security teams, IT teams, management, and other stakeholders within the organization. The reports are typically delivered via email or a secure portal, and they may also be integrated with security tools, such as firewalls and intrusion detection systems, to provide real-time protection against emerging threats. It is important to note that CTI Daily Reports are just one component of a comprehensive CTI program. The reports should be integrated with other CTI initiatives, such as threat intelligence feeds, security incident response plans, and threat hunting activities, to provide a comprehensive and effective defense against cyber threats.

CTI Daily Reports play an essential role in helping organizations stay informed about the latest cyber threats and to take proactive measures to protect their assets. The timely and relevant information provided by these reports enables organizations to maintain an assertive posture regarding cybersecurity, helping to mitigate the risk of security incidents.

Flash Reports

CTI flash reports are specially designed to be a quick and easy-to-consume source of information for decision-makers within an organization. These reports provide a concise overview of the latest and most pressing cyber threats, along with a risk assessment, impact analysis, and recommendations for mitigation. This information is crucial in helping organizations respond to emerging threats in a timely and effective manner.

23 March 2021

Alert Number

CU-000143-MW

The following information is being provided by the FBI, with no guarantees or warranties, for potential use at the sole discretion of recipients in order to protect against cyber threats. This data is provided to help cyber security professionals and system administrators' guard against the persistent malicious actions of cyber actors. This FLASH was coordinated with DHS-CISA.

This FLASH has been released TLP:WHITE. Subject to standard copyright rules, TLP:WHITE information may be distributed without restriction.

Mamba Ransomware Weaponizing DiskCryptor

Summary

Mamba ransomware has been deployed against local governments, public transportation agencies, legal services, technology services, industrial, commercial, manufacturing, and construction businesses.

Reference: https://www.cisa.gov/sites/default/files/publications/Mamba%20Flash.pdf

CTI flash reports typically include information such as:

- A brief description of the threat, including its origin, targets, and potential impact.
- An assessment of the likelihood and potential impact of the threat.
- Recommendations for mitigating the threat risk, including specific courses of action.
- Information about the credibility and reliability of the source of the intelligence.

The rapid dissemination of CTI flash reports helps organizations stay ahead of the threat landscape, which is of utmost importance in fast-moving threat environments where the risk of an attack can changes rapidly. These reports provide organizations with a succinct and actionable summary of the threat, which includes a detailed description of the threat, an assessment of its likelihood and potential impact, and recommendations for risk mitigation. This information enables organizations to prioritize their response and allocate resources, accordingly, reducing the risk of the threat and improving their overall security posture.

These reports can provide organizations with valuable insights into the source of the threat and the credibility of the information. This information can be used to improve the organization's understanding of the threat landscape and inform future CTI collection and analysis activities. This, in turn, can help organizations better prepare for and respond to future threats.

In conclusion, CTI flash reports are an essential component of a comprehensive CTI program, providing organizations with real-time and actionable information to respond to emerging cyber threats. By staying ahead of the threat landscape and having access to relevant and actionable information, organizations can reduce the risk of cyber threats and enhance their overall security posture.

Technical and Tactical Reports

Cyber Threat Intelligence (CTI) reports playing a crucial role in providing organizations with an in-depth understanding of emerging cyber threats. These reports provide a comprehensive analysis of the various elements of cyber threats, including the identification of threat actors, their tactics, techniques, and procedures (TTPs), malware analysis, reverse engineering, intrusion detection, and exploitation techniques. This information is critical for security teams and engineers who need to understand the technical aspects of a threat to determine the appropriate mitigating controls to implement.

Technical CTI reports are specifically designed for a technical audience and provide a detailed analysis of the technical aspects of a threat. These reports include information on the tools and techniques used by threat actors, the potential impact of the threat on an organization's systems, and recommendations on how to mitigate the threat effectively. Technical CTI reports are essential for IT and security professionals who need to have a deep understanding of the technical details of a threat in order to prevent an attack.

For example, a technical CTI report on a specific ransomware attack might include debugging information, hexadecimal data, and details on the different components of a file, such as a file hash, file type, threads, and associated detections. This information is valuable to malware analysts and virtual engineers who can use it to construct complex content that will help prevent current and future infections from the same or similar threats within an organization's infrastructure.

Tactical CTI reports, on the other hand, are designed for a non-technical audience and provide a high-level overview of the threat landscape. These reports provide information on the likelihood of a threat, its potential impact, and the resources required to mitigate it. They are intended for executives and business leaders who need to understand the strategic implications of a threat to make informed decisions about the organization's security posture.

Both technical and tactical CTI reports are crucial for organizations to respond effectively to emerging cyber threats. Technical reports provide the necessary technical details to mitigate the threat, while tactical reports provide the strategic context required to allocate resources effectively. By combining the information contained in both reports, organizations can develop a comprehensive understanding of the threat landscape and take the necessary steps to protect their assets and data.

Dossiers

The primary purpose of Cyber Threat Intelligence (CTI) dossiers is to provide organizations with the intelligence they need to make informed decisions about mitigating the impact of specific cyber threats. Dossiers contain comprehensive details regarding entities, subjects, or groups that pose a potential threat to your organization and play a vital role in safeguarding your organization's assets and reputation.

The information stored in CTI dossiers includes details about the threat actors and their tactics, techniques, and procedures (TTPs). This information is essential for organizations to stay ahead of the threat landscape and proactively defend against future attacks. By having a comprehensive view of the cyber threats and the actors behind them, organizations can develop effective strategies to defend against these threats and reduce the risk of a successful attack.

Summary:

Description:

Sharon Speals is suspected of attempting to recruit corporate insiders. In exchange for various sums of money, the insiders are typically required to provide credentials for access, provide sensitive data, or plant malware/ransomware.

Timeline of Activities:

Date:	Description:
02/18/2014	Community Groups first identified this actor attempting to gain access to a telco provider.
08/02/2016	Campaigns have been detected targeting the industry in order to distribute malware.
05/29/2017	Incident was a direct attack against our organizations where malware was identified, and known to be used by this actor.
11/14/2019	Another Incident was a direct attack targeting our organization, yet using and more modern version of the malware. Added evasion techniques have been implemented.
07/31/2021	A third Incident was a direct attack targeting our organization, yet using and more modern version of the malware. Added evasion techniques have been implemented.

Personal Details:

Name:	Sharon Speals	Married:	
Alias' / Handles	SpealsHoney1993		
Personal Website:	N/A	Languages:	English
Email Address:	SpealsHoney1993@gmail.com	Home Address:	(111) 222-4444
Date or Birth:	March 28th, 1993	Previous Address:	(111) 222-3333
Countries Lived In:	Canada	Cell Number:	(111) 222-5555

Social Media:

Twitter:	https://twitter.com/SpealsHoney1993
LinkedIn:	https://Linkedin.com/SpealsHoney1993
FaceBook:	https://FaceBook.com/SpealsHoney1993

CTI dossiers typically include information such as:

- **Threat actor profile:** Detailed information about the individuals or organizations behind the cyber threat, including their motivations, tactics, techniques, procedures (TTPs), and known infrastructure.

- **Threat vectors:** The specific methods or pathways used by the threat actors to penetrate the target network or systems.

- **Indicators of Compromise (IOCs):** Specific technical indicators can be used to detect the presence of the threat in the target environment.

- **Mitigation strategies:** Recommendations for mitigating the threat, including specific Courses of Action (COAs) and technical controls that can be implemented.

- **Historical data:** A historical record of previous instances of the threat, including details of the attack, the outcome, and any lessons learned.

CTI dossiers are a vital component of a strong cyber security posture for any organization. By centralizing information about cyber threats and their actors, these dossiers provide organizations with the means to make informed decisions, stay ahead of the constantly evolving threat landscape, and effectively manage cyber security risks. A comprehensive CTI program that includes the use of CTI dossiers is crucial for organizations seeking to safeguard their digital assets and defend against the ever-changing threat environment.

Requests for Information (RFI)

The CTI program should have the capability to gather and analyze intelligence from a wide range of sources and use it to develop an informed response to emerging threats. This is where RFIs play a crucial role. By sending RFIs to various sources, the CTI team can gather information about new threats and the latest trends in the cybersecurity landscape. This information can then be used to improve the accuracy of threat intelligence, identify potential targets, and develop proactive measures to mitigate the threat. For example, if the CTI team receives information about a new type of malware that is being used to attack a specific type of system, they can send an RFI to the vendor of that system to find out what measures they have put in place to protect their customers.

It is also important to consider the communication aspect of RFIs. The CTI team must ensure that the RFIs they send are well-written, clear, and concise. The recipients of the RFIs must understand what information is being sought, and the CTI team must establish clear communication channels to ensure that the information is shared in a timely and effective manner. To achieve this, it is recommended that the CTI team establish agreements with the recipients of RFIs that outline the expected response time and the methods of communication.

RFIs are crucial to the CTI process because they allow the CTI team to gather information from multiple sources, including those that have expertise in specific areas. This information will help to improve the accuracy of the threat intelligence and inform the development of practical courses of action (COAs) in response to emerging cyber threats. It is important to note that RFIs must be well-written and communicated effectively. The accuracy and quality of the information gathered will depend on the clarity of the request and the recipient's understanding of what information is being sought. To ensure that information is shared in a timely and effective manner, the CTI team should establish clear communication channels and agreements with the recipients of RFIs.

RFIs are a vital component of the CTI program, and their importance cannot be overstated. By gathering information from multiple sources, RFIs help the CTI team to stay informed about emerging cyber threats and make well-informed decisions to mitigate them. The effectiveness of RFIs will depend on the quality of the requests, the clarity of the communication, and the ability of the CTI team to analyze the information gathered and use it to inform the development of practical COAs.

Communication Plans

A comprehensive Cyber Threat Intelligence (CTI) Communication Plan should be a well-defined and documented process that outlines the procedures for sharing the intelligence gathered by the CTI team with relevant stakeholders. Regular review and updates of the plan are crucial to ensure that it stays relevant and effective in addressing the organization's changing needs and objectives.

The plan should clearly specify the preferred methods of communication, such as email, phone calls, or in-person meetings, and the frequency of communication, whether it be daily, weekly, or monthly updates. This helps to ensure that the information is communicated in a timely and effective manner without overwhelming the recipients with excessive information.

A CTI Communication Plan should include the following key components for each Intelligence Product and Service the CTI team produces:

- **Target audience:** This defines the stakeholders who will receive the information. The stakeholders may include internal teams such as IT, legal, and HR, as well as external partners and customers.

- **Communication method:** This outlines the various techniques used to communicate the information, such as email, pdf report, or phone call.

- **Frequency:** This defines how often the information will be communicated, such as daily, weekly, or monthly.

- **Content:** This outlines the information that will be communicated, such as intelligence reports, alerts, or updates on emerging cyber threats.

The CTI Communication Plan should also detail the type of information to be shared, including intelligence reports, alerts, and updates on emerging cyber threats. The information should be presented in a clear, concise, and easy-to-understand manner, highlighting key points, and providing actionable recommendations. The CTI team should consider the target audience and their level of understanding, as well as the need for confidentiality and security when determining the level of detail to be included in the information shared.

In the realm of cyber security, the Traffic Light Protocol (TLP) is a widely adopted system for managing and classifying sensitive information. TLP assigns a level of sensitivity to the information based on the potential consequences of its unauthorized disclosure. This standardized protocol helps organizations handle and distribute sensitive information in a responsible manner while also making it available to those who need it to defend against cyber threats.

TLP provides clear guidelines for sharing information based on its sensitivity level, ensuring that sensitive information is not disclosed to unauthorized individuals. This protects the organization's confidential data, proprietary information, and reputation while still enabling the Cyber Threat Intelligence (CTI) team to effectively communicate important information to the relevant stakeholders.

The use of TLP helps to strike a delicate balance between protecting sensitive information and ensuring that it is available to those who need it to mitigate the impact of cyber threats. This makes TLP a valuable tool for organizations looking to secure their sensitive information and maintain their operations in the face of rapidly evolving cyber threats.

The TLP classifies information into four categories:
- **Red:** This is the most sensitive information and should not be shared with anyone outside the organization.
- **Amber:** This is sensitive information that should only be shared within the organization and with trusted partners.
- **Green:** This information can be shared freely within the organization and trusted partners.
- **White:** This is publicly available information that can be shared freely.

Color	When should it be used?
TLP:RED Not for disclosure, restricted to participants only.	Sources may use TLP:RED when information cannot be effectively acted upon by additional parties, and could lead to impacts on a party's privacy, reputation, or operations if misused.
TLP:AMBER Limited disclosure, restricted to participants' organizations.	Sources may use TLP:AMBER when information requires support to be effectively acted upon, yet carries risks to privacy, reputation, or operations if shared outside of the organizations involved.
TLP:GREEN Limited disclosure, restricted to the community.	Sources may use TLP:GREEN when information is useful for the awareness of all participating organizations as well as with peers within the broader community or sector.
TLP:WHITE Disclosure is not limited.	Sources may use TLP:WHITE when information carries minimal or no foreseeable risk of misuse, in accordance with applicable rules and procedures for public release.

SOURCE: HTTPS://WWW.US-CERT.GOV/TLP

Effective communication is key in minimizing the impact of cyber threats on an organization and its stakeholders. By ensuring that the correct information is delivered to the right people at the right time, the CTI Communication Plan helps to ensure that the organization can respond to cyber threats in an efficient and effective manner.

Service Level Agreements (SLAs)

Service Level Agreements (SLAs) are crucial for guaranteeing the quality and consistency of Cyber Threat Intelligence (CTI) products and services. SLAs set clear expectations for service delivery and help ensure the CTI team provides a high-quality service that meets the needs of the organization. This leads to improved trust and credibility with customers, who can be confident in the level of service they receive. By defining delivery parameters, SLAs provide a framework for the CTI team to follow, promoting consistency and quality in service delivery.

Another benefit of SLAs is that they provide estimated timelines for the delivery of CTI services and products. This helps stakeholders to manage their expectations and plan accordingly during security incidents or events. By aligning the CTI team's efforts with the organization's needs, SLAs ensure that the CTI team delivers a service that provides value to the organization.

It's important to note that each product and service offered by the CTI team will have unique SLAs based on the effort required to produce and distribute the intelligence. This may include factors such as the availability of information, the complexity of analysis and production, and the distribution methods. By establishing these SLAs, the CTI team ensures that stakeholders are informed and aware of expected delivery times, which helps to mitigate risk and strengthen the organization's security posture.

In addition, SLAs help to ensure that the CTI team has the necessary resources and support to deliver their services effectively. By establishing clear expectations for the delivery of CTI services, SLAs help to ensure that the CTI team has access to the tools, personnel, and support they need to deliver their products and services to the highest possible standard. This, in turn, helps to enhance the organization's security posture and reduce the risk of cyber threats.

SLAs are a critical component of a successful CTI program. By providing stakeholders with a clear understanding of the delivery times for intelligence products, SLAs help to enhance the organization's overall security posture, enable informed decisions and appropriate actions to be taken during security incidents or events and strengthen the relationship between the CTI team and their customers.

Action Items

For each intelligence requirement that has been established, complete the Service Catalogue, Courses-of-Action, Communication Plans, and Service Level Agreements (SLAs) section.

Details should include but not be limited to the following:

Service Catalogue:
- Determine what type of products can be produced based on the Intelligence Requirements, intelligence sources, and COAs.
- Determine what tools and teams may leverage these services and products and what formats are to be used:
  - **Example:** CSVs, STIX bundles, PDF reports, emails, and other communications
- Determine how frequently these services and products can be produced.
- Add the service catalog components to the appropriate use cases.

Courses of Action (COAs)
- Identify your organization's capabilities to determine where threat intelligence can be leveraged.
  - **Examples:** IOCs and detection rules to IDS/IPS or SIEM, phishing Take-down requests, configuration updates and hardening efforts, external/internal reporting
- Identify key contacts and Subject Matter Experts (SMEs) within your organization who can be contacted for more information about their area of expertise and other internal operations.
- Identify online tools and portals that can be used for reporting malicious or suspicious content or activity.

- Ensure each COA has associated classification and applicable Courses-of-Action (COAs).

Communication Plans
- Identify distribution lists, stakeholders, key contacts who are to be recipients of CTI products and services.
- Request feedback on intelligence products delivered to ensure they are meeting and exceeding the expectation of your stakeholders.

Service Level Agreements (SLAs)
- Establish SLAs for the production and distribution of each intelligence product.
- Leverage templates, scripts, or other automation to produce consistent CTI products.
- Objective is to have the lowest SLA as possible.

When the intelligence requirements sections for these have been completed the IRs should look like the image to the below.

Service Catalogue:			
	Products:	Recipients:	SLAs:
Strategic:	• Flash Report	• Security Managers, C-Level team	• 4 hrs
Operational:	• Vulnerability Hunting	• VM Team	• 1 hr
Tactical:	• Detection Signatures	• SIEM	• 2 hrs
Summary of Activities:			
Upon the detection of a Zero-day or critical vulnerability within a technology within our organization the Cyber-Threat Intelligence Team will, first search the environment to determine is the organization is exposed. If yes, the CTI Team will produce strategic reporting in the form of a Flash Notification to the Security Manager, C-Level team advising them of the situation and what is currently being done by the security and intelligence team. In addition to this the CTI will attempt to produce detection capabilities such as IOC threat feeds, and snort signatures to be able to detect/block potentially malicious traffic.			
Risk Reducing Courses of Action (CoAs):			
Discover:	• Threat Hunting activities within the SIEM to determine if the organization may potentially already be compromised. • Vulnerability hunting activities to determine is the organization is exposed to the vulnerabilities.		
Detect:	• Implement detection rules and signatures in order to be alerted in the event of newly		
Deny:	• Blacklist IOCs including Domains, URLs and file hashes within the next-gen firewall		
Disrupt:	• Report malicious activity to the threat actors ISP for take-down • Submit IOCs to online reputation databases.		
Degrade:	• N/A		
Deceive:	• N/A		
Destroy:	• N/A		

It is important to keep track of changes to your intelligence requirements, especially as they evolve and become more complex over time. By updating the relevant documents to reflect these changes, you can ensure that everyone involved is aware of the most recent information and requirements. A "version history" or "revision log" provides a record of these changes and can help track the progression of your intelligence requirements over time. This can be particularly useful for understanding the context of a particular change and why it was made, as well as for identifying any patterns or trends in the evolution of your requirements. Keeping a clear and well-documented record of changes can help support better decision-making and collaboration within your organization.

Summary

In this chapter, we covered the key elements that support a Threat Intelligence (CTI) team's effort, such as courses of action, a service catalog, communication plans, and service level agreements. We discussed how to identify what courses of action the CTI team can take, classify these courses of action, and measure the strength of the organization's defenses against emerging cyber threats. We also discussed setting up communication plans for each product or service offered, determining who should receive them and how, and implementing service level agreements for each product or service provided. The CTI team also created a service catalog of the services they offer.

Now that the foundational elements have been covered, the focus can shift to the tools used to assist and automate the collection and processing of information. The next chapter will cover various intelligence tools to ensure that information is consistently and efficiently collected. These tools can automate certain tasks, serve as a data repository for referencing historical findings and actions, and support operational reporting and metrics. This concludes the chapter on intelligence requirements, and the focus will shift to intelligence tools in the following chapter.

Chapter #5 - Intelligence Tools

Introduction

The Intelligence Tool phase is a crucial component of implementing a Cyber Threat Intelligence (CTI) program. During this phase, we use the intelligence requirements established in previous stages to determine the operational tools, data repositories, and sources necessary for realizing these requirements. This allows us to define the technical specifications needed to support the intelligence requirements, including hardware and software, licenses, and subscriptions.

Our focus in this phase is to identify the intelligence tools necessary for collecting, storing, and processing data and examine how they can work with other security tools and data sources. This is essential to ensure that the CTI program can effectively collect, store, and analyze data and provide actionable intelligence to protect against cyber threats.

Intelligence tools	• Determine tools to collect, store, & process data. • Understand how various intelligence tools can integrate with each other as well as other security tools, or data sources. • Determine technical dependencies to support CTI tools.
Operational metrics and reporting	• Measure performance of the overall CTI program • Provide insight into the overall threat landscape. • Identify operational metrics and reporting to measure performance and effectiveness of the CTI team and their Courses-of-Action. • Determine required data and where to collect this.

The information gathered in this phase is then used in the subsequent chapter, focused on operational metrics and reporting, where we will measure the performance of the CTI program, gain insights into the threat landscape, and determine metrics to assess cyber threat risk and internal risk reduction. By choosing the necessary data and its sources, we ensure that the CTI program has the information it needs to effectively protect against cyber threats.

Chapter Objectives

Upon completion of this chapter, participants will have the knowledge to select the appropriate tools that are required to support the functions of a Cyber Threat Intelligence Team.

- Determine appropriate tools that can be used to support the operations of the Cyber-Threat Intelligence team.
- Estimate cost requirements for hardware, software, and other dependencies associated with various tools and intelligence requirements.
- Understand the basic concepts of Operational Security (OPSEC) and how your investigative actions may provide forewarning to a threat actor.
- Discuss the benefits and capabilities of commonly used Threat Intelligence Platforms (TIPs).
- Compare and contrast the benefits and disadvantages of using online resources and services.

Data Collection

A comprehensive and thorough approach is crucial when building a Cyber Threat Intelligence (CTI) program. The success of the CTI program depends on the proper assessment of data sources and the methods used to collect the data, based on the specific intelligence requirements. The first step in this process is to analyze the format and structure of the data source, determining the best way to manage the information. For instance, if the data source is available in a structured format, such as a pre-populated CSV file, it can be integrated directly into the CTI system. This is the case for some threat feeds that use the STIX and TAXII protocols, which allow for seamless integration of data into a Security Information and Event Management (SIEM) system.

In contrast, some data sources may require manual collection efforts, such as visiting websites or logging into applications. In such cases, the focus is on how to manipulate, automate, and parse the data, and whether manual or automated methods should be used. The tools used for data collection play a critical role in the selection of data sources, as some sources may need to be available in a specific format. For instance, if a website does not have an RSS feed or email alert, custom scripting may be necessary to scrape specific page content on a regular basis.

It is essential to have alternative sources of data to ensure the resilience of the CTI program. This redundancy in data sources allows the CTI team to monitor other sites and collect the same information, thereby maintaining continuity of operations even if a website is down. This also ensures that the CTI program can continue to provide its services and act on intelligence requirements even if a system or feed fails.

In conclusion, a successful CTI program requires a thorough assessment of data sources, careful analysis of the format and structure of the data, and a robust approach to data collection based on the intelligence requirements. The use of alternative sources of data is crucial to ensure the resilience of the program and the continuity of operations.

Data Pull

Cyber Threat Intelligence (CTI) is a critical aspect of modern cybersecurity practices. To provide effective intelligence, the CTI team needs access to a variety of data sources. These data sources can include internal network logs, external threat intelligence feeds, social media, and open-source intelligence, among others. The challenge lies in receiving and processing this data from various locations in a timely and efficient manner.

This is where the concept of pulling data comes into play. Pulling data involves manually acquiring data from different sources, including open-source intelligence (OSINT) sources such as online forums and social media platforms, as well as internal sources like network logs and traffic data. This method allows organizations to gather a more diverse and representative set of data, providing a more accurate view of the potential threat.

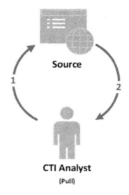

Source

1   2

CTI Analyst
(Pull)

Pulling data can also be automated, reducing the risk of human error and saving time and resources. Automated data collection can be performed regularly, ensuring that the most up-to-date information is always available for analysis. This enables organizations to respond quickly to emerging threats without the need for manual data gathering. In cases where the desired data is downloadable from a website, such as a regularly updated CSV file, automated data collection can be performed with ease.

Example: A simple 2-line linux bash script could easily accomplish this:

```
#!/bin/bash
curl http://example.com/file.csv -o file.csv
```

The pulling data concept is straightforward and portable, making it easy for analysts to access and gather data regardless of the system they use. The sources are typically located on the internet or within the organization's environment, making it simple for analysts to access and gather the information they need. However, for large organizations with many data sources, manual data collection can be time-consuming and may require synchronization of updates between analysts.

Pulling data is a crucial aspect of a cyber threat intelligence program. By gathering data from various sources and integrating it, organizations can create a comprehensive view of the cyber threat landscape, enabling them to make informed decisions about their security posture. Automated data collection can provide organizations with real-time visibility into emerging threats and trends, while reducing the risk of human error and saving time and resources.

Data Push

Push notifications in Cyber Threat Intelligence (CTI) are an indispensable tool for organizations to stay informed about emerging cyber threats in real-time. These notifications provide timely and efficient updates and alerts to the CTI team, saving valuable time and effort that would otherwise be spent on manual checking.

To maximize the benefits of push notifications, it is essential to centralize them and send them to a shared mailbox, email distribution list, or a centralized platform. This ensures that all members of the CTI team have access to the latest information, reducing the risk of operational issues and data loss in the event of staff turnover.

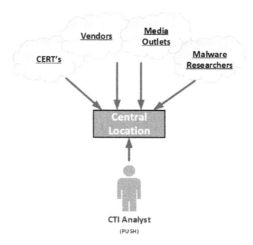

Having a centralized location for the data also helps to maintain a consistent view of the cyber threat landscape across the organization. This enhances collaboration among the CTI team, reduces the risk of operational issues, and improves the overall security posture of the organization. A consistent view of the data also ensures that everyone in the organization has a clear understanding of the current cyber threat environment, reducing the risk of a successful attack.

Web Searching

When conducting online investigations, search engines can be a valuable tool in identifying potential threat intelligence data sources. Search engines can narrow down the search results by using specific keywords or phrases and help analysts quickly locate relevant information. However, it is essential to note that not all search engines are created equal. Each search engine has its algorithms that prioritize websites differently and may return different results for the same query. Therefore, it is crucial to carefully consider which search engine you are using and how this could impact your search results.

For example, some search engines prioritize popular websites, while others prioritize more obscure or lesser-known sources. Additionally, some search engines may more effectively identify specific data types, such as social media posts or forum discussions. In contrast, other search engines may be better suited for identifying technical information, such as vulnerabilities or malware.

Search engines can significantly support a Cyber Threat Intelligence (CTI) program by helping to collect data and narrow down sources for review. By using various search operators and refining search queries, search engines can improve the efficiency of web searches and provide better results. With the help of search engines, cybersecurity professionals can identify potential threats and vulnerabilities, analyze their characteristics, and take appropriate measures to prevent them from causing harm. Therefore, cybersecurity professionals must be proficient in using search engines and web browsers for effective CTI program implementation.

Browser Bookmarks

Organizing bookmarks into folders is a fundamental technique used by CTI professionals to manage and categorize data sources effectively. Categorizing bookmarks based on specific topics or areas of focus enables CTI professionals to access relevant information easily and quickly. This saves time and ensures that the necessary information can be easily retrieved.

However, more than categorizing bookmarks into folders alone is required. Regularly reviewing and updating bookmarks is crucial to ensure that the information collected remains current and relevant to the CTI program's objectives. Since threat actors and their tactics are constantly evolving, CTI professionals must regularly update their bookmarks to ensure they have the latest information. Please update bookmarks to avoid collecting outdated information, which could be counterproductive and affect the CTI program's effectiveness.

Besides essential bookmark management, tools like browser extensions or bookmark managers can enhance the CTI program's data collection capabilities. These tools can provide additional features like saving page content and metadata, making it easier to search and review saved data later. This can improve the efficiency and effectiveness of the CTI program by enabling quick and easy retrieval of important information.

Email Alerts

Email alerts are a valuable tool for cybersecurity professionals as they allow them to stay up to date with changes on websites that may contain critical information or vulnerabilities. These alerts are generally sent automatically when a website is updated and include a link to the new or modified content. By clicking on the link provided in the email, CTI analysts can quickly assess the nature of the change and determine if it poses a potential security threat.

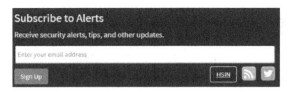

The advantage of using email alerts is that it eliminates the need for constant manual checks on multiple websites, which can be time-consuming and inefficient. Instead, analysts can use email client rules and workflows to automate the process of filtering, flagging, and categorizing alerts based on specific keywords or other criteria. This helps streamline the collection and analysis process and makes it easier to identify potential threats or trends in real-time.

By applying these rules, analysts can prioritize alerts based on their level of importance and quickly respond to critical threats. This can be particularly useful in cases where immediate action is required, such as a significant data breach or cyber-attack.

RSS Feeds

RSS (Really Simple Syndication) feeds a valuable addition to any Cyber Threat Intelligence (CTI) program. They allow you to collect data automatically from various websites and store it in one centralized location. By subscribing to multiple feeds, you can quickly gather a large amount of information from different sources, which can be easily implemented using an RSS client. Many email clients, such as Microsoft Outlook and Mozilla Thunderbird, offer RSS capabilities, making it easy to receive updates like regular emails.

One of the primary benefits of using RSS feeds in a CTI program is the reduction of time and effort required to collect data manually. This tool streamlines the data collection process, allowing you to track the latest threats and landscape developments. Furthermore, RSS feeds can efficiently track and monitor specific topics of interest, such as malware, phishing, or zero-day vulnerabilities. By subscribing to feeds from sources that provide information on particular types of threats, you can receive updates in real-time as new information becomes available.

Incorporating RSS feeds into a CTI program can help you collect and analyze a large amount of information from multiple sources and stay informed on the latest developments in the threat landscape. When using RSS feeds as part of your CTI program, you must consider the reliability and accuracy of the information you are collecting. To ensure the quality of your intelligence, it's recommended to use multiple sources and validate data before acting on it.

Tweet Deck (Twitter)

Leveraging social media monitoring tools like TweetDeck can be immensely beneficial for collecting and analyzing data for a cyber threat intelligence program. TweetDeck is a powerful social media monitoring tool that displays live updates from Twitter in a columnar format, making it easier to track multiple accounts, hashtags, and searches simultaneously. This tool helps monitor real-time updates on potential threats, such as new vulnerabilities, data breaches, and cyber-attacks.

Using TweetDeck, cyber security professionals can monitor hashtags related to emerging cyber threats, allowing them to quickly identify potential issues and take proactive measures to mitigate them. Moreover, the desktop version of TweetDeck is recommended for its wider display of data, making it easier to scan through updates and identify potential threats. By dedicating a separate monitor for TweetDeck, professionals can ensure that they have a comprehensive overview of the latest developments.

In addition to monitoring potential threats, using TweetDeck can also help cybersecurity professionals identify trending topics related to cybersecurity. This includes the latest industry news, best practices, and emerging threats. Cybersecurity professionals can better understand the evolving threat landscape and take necessary steps to protect their organization by keeping an eye on these trends.

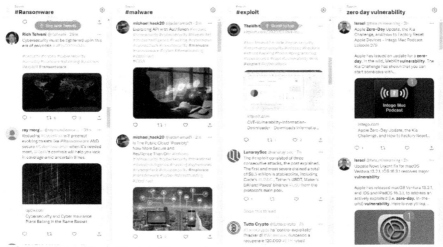

Reference: https://TweetDeck.twitter.com/

TweetDeck can support a Cyber Threat Intelligence (CTI) program for data collection in several ways:

- **Monitoring keywords:** TweetDeck allows you to create columns that track specific keywords, hashtags, or handles. This feature can monitor topics of interest to your CTI programs, such as specific cyber threats, vulnerabilities, or actors.

- **Filtering content:** TweetDeck provides advanced filtering options, such as location, language, and source that can be used to refine the data you collect. This allows you to focus on relevant content and minimize noise.

- **Automated collection:** TweetDeck supports data collection through APIs and integrations with other tools, such as Hootsuite or Zapier. This allows you to set up automatic data collection workflows, freeing up time for analysis and response.

- **Collaboration:** TweetDeck allows multiple users to access and collaborate on the same columns and feeds, making it a valuable tool for teams working on CTI. Teams can share information and collaborate on responses, increasing the efficiency and effectiveness of their CTI program.

- **Real-time updates:** TweetDeck provides real-time updates, making it an ideal tool for collecting and monitoring fast-paced, time-sensitive information. This can be particularly useful for tracking emerging threats and vulnerabilities.

Monitoring multiple hashtags or search criteria in real-time using TweetDeck can provide valuable insights into cyber criminals' behavior and tactics, helping organizations identify emerging threats and respond to them accordingly. In addition to improving incident response, having a live dashboard of Twitter updates can also help identify trending topics related to cybersecurity and stay up to date on the latest developments and best practices.

Commercial Vendors and Platforms

By leveraging the tools and services offered by commercial vendors, organizations can efficiently collect and analyze data for their CTI program, which can help to streamline the data management process, saving time and effort. This integration also allows for seamless compatibility with a company's current security infrastructure, enabling the organization to improve the efficiency and effectiveness of its CTI products and services.

In addition to providing tools and services, commercial vendors can also offer access to a team of experts who are knowledgeable about the latest cybersecurity threats and trends. This expertise level can help organizations avoid emerging risks and effectively mitigate potential threats.

Another advantage of working with commercial vendors is scalability. As an organization grows, its needs and the threat landscape will evolve, and the CTI program should be adjusted and scaled accordingly. Commercial vendors can offer scalable solutions that allow organizations to adapt and grow their CTI program to manage new and emerging risks effectively.

These vendors and services can offer access to a wide range of data sources, including:

- **Threat Intelligence Feeds:** Commercial vendors can provide access to real-time feeds of threat intelligence data, including information on new and emerging threats, attack methods, and malware samples.

- **Threat Intelligence Platforms:** Vendors can offer integrated platforms that allow organizations to collect, store, and analyze vast amounts of threat intelligence data from multiple sources, including their networks and the open-source intelligence community.

- **Threat Intelligence Analytics:** Commercial vendors can provide advanced analytics tools and services to help organizations make sense of the vast amount of data collected, including machine learning and artificial intelligence, to identify patterns and trends in threat activity.

- **Managed Services:** Organizations can also outsource their CTI program to commercial vendors who offer managed services, which can include ongoing threat monitoring, data collection, and analysis.

Integrating with commercial vendors can be a valuable strategy for organizations seeking to optimize their CTI program. By leveraging their expertise, tools, and services, companies can efficiently collect and analyze data, stay ahead of emerging risks, and adapt to changing needs and the evolving threat landscape.

Intelligence Tools

The tools required for a CTI program typically include data collection, research, investigation, and tracking systems. These tools are necessary to gather intelligence on potential threats, analyze data, and track the progress of investigations. To ensure that these tools are practical and effective, it is crucial to select those that are well-suited to the organization's technical, business, and intelligence needs. It is also essential to choose tools that can integrate with other tools through API calls or similar mechanisms. This will allow the tools to work together and provide a comprehensive source of data and information, enabling the organization to make informed decisions about the potential threats they face.

When choosing CTI tools, it is possible to use both open-source and commercial options. However, there are various factors to consider, including where the tools will reside (on premise or in the cloud), how they will be accessed and secured, and who will support them. For example, organizations may choose to use on premise tools for enhanced security, but cloud-based solutions may provide greater flexibility and scalability. It is also essential to identify any potential risks these tools may pose to the organization and to take appropriate measures to mitigate them.

In the case of SaaS services, it is important to consider data protection and privacy issues. Organizations need to ensure that data is adequately protected, and that the service provider is not using the data to enhance their offerings further. Additionally, licensing requirements, technical dependencies, and automation capabilities should be considered before implementing any CTI tools.

On-Premise Install	SaaS Service
• How will the tool be accessed and secured • Could the installation of these tools pose a risk to your organization? • Who and how will these tools be support?	• How will you integrate/interface with a service? • How is your data being protected, and who is responsible? • Is the service provider using your data to support their service offering (privacy issues)?

It is also vital to test CTI tools in a safe and secure environment per organizational policies and procedures. This will enable organizations to identify and address potential issues before deploying the tools in a production environment. When downloading and installing software, especially open-source tools, it is crucial to exercise caution and ensure that the tools have been peer-reviewed for malicious content.

In conclusion, building a successful CTI program requires carefully considering the tools, services, subscriptions, and portals required to support its operations. Cybersecurity professionals need to evaluate these tools based on various factors, including location, security, data protection, licensing, technical dependencies, and automation capabilities. By testing these tools in a safe and secure environment and following organizational policies and procedures, organizations can build a comprehensive CTI program to protect against cyber threats.

Data Collection and Enrichment

Cyber Threat Intelligence (CTI) is a comprehensive and multifaceted approach to cyber security that is crucial for any organization operating in the digital age. It is a process that involves the systematic collection, analysis, and utilization of information related to existing and emerging cyber threats. This information can help organizations to identify potential risks and proactively implement security measures to mitigate those risks.

CTI programs collect data from various sources, including open-source intelligence, threat intelligence feeds, malware sandboxes, and log management and analysis tools. By analyzing this data, organizations can identify trends, tactics, and indicators of compromise (IOCs) associated with cyber threats. This analysis helps organizations anticipate potential threats and proactively implement security measures to mitigate those risks.

One of the primary benefits of a CTI program is its ability to provide a centralized view of cyber threat intelligence data. This allows organizations to identify and respond to threats quickly. Additionally, data collection and analysis automation help reduce the workload on security teams and improve the overall efficiency of the CTI program.

However, it is essential to note that CTI is only one component of a comprehensive cybersecurity program. Although CTI provides valuable insights into the evolving threat landscape, it should be combined with other security controls to ensure the overall security and resilience of the organization. CTI should be used with firewalls, intrusion detection systems, endpoint protection, and other security measures to provide complete defense against cyber threats.

Local Applications

Below are some examples of freely available tools that can be installed locally and used for data collection and enrichment capabilities:

- Maltego - Integrate data from public sources (OSINT), commercial vendors, and internal sources to establish links and other data correlations.
- Recon-ng - Recon-ng provides a powerful environment in which open-source web-based reconnaissance can be conducted, and we can gather all information.
- theHarvester - TheHarvester is a command-line tool included in Kali Linux that acts as a wrapper for a variety of search engines and is used to find email accounts, subdomain names, virtual hosts, open ports / banners, and employee names related to a domain from different public sources (such as search engines and PGP key servers).
- Shodan (CLI) - Shodan is a search engine that lets users search for various types of servers (also has a Command Line Version).
- Metagoofil - Metagoofil is an information gathering tool designed for extracting metadata of public documents (pdf, doc, xls, ppt, docx, pptx, xlsx) belonging to a target company.
- SpiderFoot - SpiderFoot is unique in that it recursively analyses each piece of data found during a scan so that no stone is left unturned.

Online Applications

Below are some examples of freely available online intelligence services that can be used for data collection and enrichment capabilities:

- VirusTotal - VirusTotal is a free virus, malware, and URL online scanning service.
- Whois.sc - Research domain ownership with Whois Lookup: Get ownership info, IP address history, rank, traffic, SEO & more. Find available domains & domains for sale.
- URLscan.io - Website scanner for suspicious and malicious URLs.
- Shodan.io - Shodan is a search engine that lets users search for various types of servers connected to the internet using a variety of filters. Some have also described it as a search engine of service banners, which are metadata that the server sends back to the client.
- App.Any.Run - Online malware analysis tools you can research malicious files and URLs and get result with incredible speed
- Hybrid-Analysis - Submit malware for free analysis with Falcon Sandbox and Hybrid Analysis technology.
- Intelligence X - Intelligence X is a search engine and data archive. Search Tor, I2P, data leaks and the public web by email, domain, IP, CIDR, Bitcoin address and more.

Please Note: When using these online services, you are the product. For example, if you use an online malware sandbox, your analysis results will most likely be available to you and any other service user. If you are sandboxing sensitive files, this may lead to a new information disclosure issue.

Before using any of these services, it is best to review their terms and conditions to fully understand what will be done with your data while using their services.

Tracking Systems

Cyber Threat Intelligence (CTI) tracking systems and repositories are critical components of a comprehensive CTI program. They are used to store and manage the vast amount of data generated and consumers to support CTI efforts, providing a centralized location for storing and organizing threat intelligence information. These tracking tools also allow organizations to categorize and prioritize threat intelligence data based on their specific requirements and risk profile. This capability enables them to identify and respond to the most critical threats and prioritize their security efforts accordingly.

The various platforms used for tracking CTI activities often come with collaboration and sharing features that allow organizations to share intelligence with other organizations and stakeholders, improving the effectiveness of the CTI program. They also support the automation of sharing threat intelligence data with other security tools and systems, such as firewalls, intrusion detection systems, and endpoint protection. This automation ensures that all security systems receive the necessary intelligence data, enabling them to detect and respond to potential threats effectively.

These tracking tools also support reporting and metrics, enabling organizations to measure the effectiveness of their CTI program. By analyzing the data collected through these systems, organizations can generate reports that show the number of threats detected and blocked, the types of threats, and the success rate of their mitigation efforts. These reports provide valuable insights that help organizations refine their CTI program continually.

Excel

For small to medium-sized organizations, spreadsheet programs are a commonly used tool for tracking and organizing IOCs due to their data manipulation and filtering capabilities, making them an efficient and user-friendly option. However, exercising caution when working with IOCs in spreadsheet applications is essential, as the links may be live and compromise the system if clicked.

Submitted	IP	Flag	Country	Description
10/4/2020 14:09	45.142.120.31	IR	Iran	SMTP auth brute force
10/4/2020 14:09	45.142.120.32	IR	Iran	SMTP auth brute force
10/4/2020 14:09	120.79.188.144	CN	China	FTP auth brute force
10/4/2020 14:09	101.89.116.39	CN	China	FTP auth brute force
10/4/2020 16:42	83.97.20.31	RO	Romania	Port scanning
10/4/2020 20:41	222.186.30.218	CN	China	SSH malicious
10/5/2020 7:40	139.162.247.102	GB	United Kingdom	SSH malicious
10/7/2020 6:41	82.102.16.195	DE	Germany	FTP auth brute force
10/7/2020 6:41	103.78.242.69	MY	Malaysia	slothfulmedia malware
10/7/2020 6:41	122.51.173.33	CN	China	FTP auth brute force
10/8/2020 9:00	198.12.66.108	US	United States	AgentTesla LimeRat malspam
10/8/2020 13:14	31.145.137.246	TR	Turkey	FTP auth brute force

Source: https://github.com/tesla-consulting/ioc-list/blob/main/iplist.csv

To avoid this, working with IOCs in a plain text editor such as Notepad and defang the URL is recommended. Defanging involves modifying the links to prevent them from being clickable by using square brackets around periods and domain names and IP addresses (i.e., 192.168.0[.]x) or by changing the protocol of the URL to something else (i.e., hxxp://, meow://). Once the IOCs have been defanged, they can be tracked in Excel by creating a standard document that includes timestamps, IP addresses, WHOIS information, and a description of the IOC.

The document could include information such as the time the IOC was identified, the IP address, the country and short form of the country, the source you obtained this IOC from, and a description of what the IOC was associated with (e.g., port scanning, malware). Customizing the document based on your tracking requirements and including any additional data points that are important for your tracking purposes is essential.

Spreadsheets are valuable for tracking and organizing IOCs in a CTI program. Still, it is crucial to follow best practices and take necessary precautions to ensure the system's safety. This includes working with IOCs in a plain text editor, defanging URLs, and customizing the document based on your tracking requirements. By implementing these practices, you can effectively monitor and track IOCs, make informed decisions, and implement proactive measures to safeguard your organization against cyber threats.

SharePoint

SharePoint is a web-based collaboration and document management platform developed by Microsoft. It can be used as a CTI tracking system and repository by organizations looking for a centralized location to store and manage their threat intelligence data.

With SharePoint, organizations can create custom lists and libraries to store and organize threat intelligence data, such as Indicators of Compromise (IOCs) and Threat Intelligence Reports. SharePoint's user-friendly interface and customizable features allow organizations to categorize and prioritize threat intelligence data based on their specific requirements and risk profile.

SharePoint also provides collaboration features, such as discussion boards and document collaboration, allowing organizations to share threat intelligence data with other stakeholders and security teams. This can improve the overall effectiveness of the CTI program by enabling teams to share information and collaborate on responses to cyber threats. Additionally, SharePoint's integration with other Microsoft products and APIs will enable organizations to automate the sharing of threat intelligence data with other security tools and systems. For example, organizations can integrate SharePoint with their SIEM solution to automatically trigger alerts based on the threat intelligence data stored in SharePoint.

SharePoint can be used as a CTI tracking system and repository to store and manage threat intelligence data and to improve collaboration and information sharing among security teams.

Ticketing Systems

Ticketing systems are more than just simple applications that log task data. They offer a range of features that help to categorize, prioritize, and manage the courses of action taken by the CTI team. For example, these systems can tag or classify courses of action, apply Service Level Agreements (SLAs) to prioritize tasks, provide automatic and custom dashboards for data visualization, and offer API integrations for easy integration with other systems. These automation capabilities greatly assist the CTI team in maintaining and tracking the progress of their activities and courses-of-action and can also help generate reports for stakeholders.

Suppose an organization already has a ticketing system in place. In that case, it is best to utilize it to track the CTI team's courses-of-action, rather than implementing a dedicated CTI ticketing system. This allows for seamless integration with other teams and systems within the organization. In addition, the features offered by these systems, such as automation, data visualization, and data organization, can significantly aid the CTI team in responding to and mitigating cyber threats.

Ticketing systems also provide the ability to manage workflows and ensure that all tasks are completed within the deadlines. This is critical in ensuring that the CTI team is agile and responsive to emerging cyber threats. By tracking and managing workflows, the CTI team can quickly respond to threats and ensure that all necessary actions are taken to mitigate the risks.

Cyber Threat Intelligence (CTI) programs are critical for modern cyber security, and tracking and ticketing systems are essential components of an effective CTI program. These systems offer a range of features that help to categorize, prioritize, and manage courses of action taken by the CTI team, ensuring that cyber threats are effectively mitigated. Suppose an organization already has a ticketing system in place. In that case, it is best to utilize that system for tracking the CTI team's courses of action, as this allows for seamless integration with other teams and systems within the organization.

Threat Intelligence Platforms (TIP)

Cyber threats are becoming increasingly complex and sophisticated, making it challenging for organizations to defend against them effectively. TIPs offer a centralized location for collecting, analyzing, and managing threat intelligence data, enabling organizations to proactively identify and mitigate threats.

TIPs are designed to gather information from a wide range of sources, including internal security tools, open-source intelligence feeds, and other third-party providers. This information is then analyzed and correlated to identify patterns and anomalies that could indicate potential threats. The platform can also help automate the collection and analysis of threat intelligence data, allowing security teams to focus on identifying and responding to the most critical threats.

Below are some of the benefits for leveraging a TIP:
- **Data Collection:** A TIP can collect and import threat intelligence data from various sources, including open-source intelligence (OSINT), commercial threat intelligence feeds, malware sandboxes, and log management and analysis tools. This data can create a comprehensive picture of the current threat landscape and support decision-making and proactive measures.

- **Data Analysis:** The TIP can analyze the collected data to identify trends, tactics, techniques, and procedures (TTPs) associated with cyber threats, as well as Indicators of Compromise (IOCs). The TIP can also enrich the data by adding additional context and information, such as geolocation, historical data, and threat actor information.

- **Event Management:** TIPs provide event management capabilities that allow analysts to associate related information and add context to threat events. Analysts can add comments, tags, and metadata to events to provide additional information and facilitate the analysis process.

- **Threat Prioritization:** The TIP can categorize and prioritize threat intelligence data based on the organization's requirements and risk profile. This allows organizations to quickly identify and respond to the most pressing threats and prioritize their security efforts.

- **Collaboration and Sharing:** features for collaborating and sharing intelligence with other organizations and stakeholders. It supports sharing data through the STIX and TAXII protocols, allowing organizations to exchange information in a standardized and secure manner.

- **Integration with Other Security Tools:** The TIP can automate the sharing of threat intelligence data with other security tools and systems, such as firewalls, intrusion detection systems, SIEM, and endpoint protection. This integration can help organizations improve the effectiveness of their security defenses by using the latest threat intelligence to detect and respond to threats more quickly.

A TIP provides organizations with a centralized location for collecting, analyzing, and managing threat intelligence data, enabling them to prioritize and respond to cyber threats effectively. A well-designed TIP can also improve collaboration and information sharing, helping organizations stay ahead of the evolving threat landscape.

Malware Information Sharing Platform

MISP (Malware Information Sharing Platform) is an open-source platform for sharing threat intelligence and analysis between organizations, security researchers, and analysts. It is designed to store, share, and correlate cyber threat intelligence in a structured format, allowing organizations to understand better and respond to cyber threats.

One of the significant benefits of MISP is its customizability and extensibility. The platform can be tailored to an organization's specific needs and integrated into existing security infrastructure. This feature ensures that organizations can leverage MISP to their advantage without significantly changing their existing security ecosystem.

MISP allows users to share threat intelligence in various formats, including indicators of compromise (IOCs), malware samples, threat intelligence reports, and more. This wide range of collaboration features enables users to create and join communities of users with similar interests and participate in threat intelligence-sharing initiatives with other organizations. This way, users can learn from each other's experiences and expertise, thereby making it easier to detect, prevent, and respond to cyber threats more effectively.

By enabling organizations to benefit from the collective knowledge and experience of a broad community of security professionals, MISP plays a vital role in enhancing cybersecurity defenses. The more organizations use MISP to share threat intelligence, the more effective they become at detecting and preventing attacks. In summary, MISP is an essential tool for any organization looking to improve its cybersecurity posture and better protect itself against cyber threats.

OpenCTI

OpenCTI, short for Open Cyber Threat Intelligence, is an open-source Threat Intelligence Platform (TIP) that allows organizations to collect, process, and visualize threat intelligence. With OpenCTI, users can create and manage threat intelligence data, including indicators of compromise (IOCs), tactics, techniques, procedures (TTPs), and other relevant threat information. Its primary purpose is to assist organizations in understanding and mitigating cyber threats by centralizing and analyzing threat data from multiple sources.

OpenCTI offers a user-friendly web-based interface that lets users view their threat intelligence data in a visual representation. In addition, the platform provides an API that allows developers to integrate OpenCTI with other security tools like firewalls, intrusion detection systems, and Security Information and Event Management (SIEM) solutions.

One of the significant benefits of OpenCTI is its ability to pivot between entities and relationships, enabling analysts to explore the entire data set and better understand a particular threat's context. For instance, when an analyst investigates a phishing campaign, they can pivot from the phishing email to the malicious domain name, IP address, and the threat actor behind the campaign. This capability provides a comprehensive view of the threat landscape, which helps organizations respond more efficiently and effectively to cyber threats.

OpenCTI also enables organizations to share threat intelligence data with other security tools, automating the update of firewall rules to block traffic to known command and control servers, thereby preventing the spread of malware within the organization.

The platform can also be used with data visualization and correlation tools like Maltego, allowing organizations to understand the relationships and connections between events and data sources. This capability helps analysts to visualize the associations between different indicators of compromise, such as IP addresses, domain names, and file hashes, providing a clear picture of the threat landscape.

OpenCTI is a valuable tool for organizations establishing and managing a Cyber Threat Intelligence (CTI) program. It provides the necessary capabilities to store, collect, and analyze threat intelligence data, which helps improve the organization's threat defense posture. With its ability to pivot between entities and relationships, integrate with other security tools, and provide data visualization and correlation capabilities, OpenCTI is an essential tool for any CTI program.

Research and Investigations

Operational Security (OpSec)

Operational security, commonly known as OpSec, is a crucial component of a robust and effective cyber threat intelligence program. The primary goal of OpSec is to prevent adversaries from detecting and exploiting vulnerabilities in the organization's security posture. One essential method of ensuring OpSec during data collection is leveraging Virtual Private Networks (VPNs).

VPNs allow users to reroute their internet traffic through the provider's servers, making it difficult for adversaries to track their online activities. Using a VPN enables investigators to obtain a public IP address from the provider and choose the location from which their traffic originates. This helps cover the investigator's tracks and prevents the adversary from detecting their activities through logs or other fingerprints like IP addresses or user agents.

Another critical aspect of OpSec is the use of segregated infrastructure while conducting security investigations. During these investigations, it may be necessary to disable security controls to gain a complete understanding of the code or malware's intended purpose. However, disabling security controls can make the activities riskier as it opens up the possibility of unexpected results. To mitigate this risk, it is recommended to use a dedicated subnet with dedicated systems and hardware that can always be reverted to a safe state. Virtualization technologies such as VMware or VirtualBox can be used to facilitate the segregated infrastructure. This way, in the event of an infection, the virtual machine can be easily destroyed and restored from a backup, safeguarding the corporate environment.

Social media can also be a valuable tool for research and investigations, but it is critical to use it securely to prevent tipping off the adversary. It is essential to avoid using personal accounts for this purpose as it would reveal the investigator's activities. Instead, dummy social media accounts, also known as sock puppets, should be created to perform these activities. This way, any interaction is associated with fake accounts and has no affiliation with the actual analyst or the organization, ensuring the investigator's anonymity.

In a cyber threat intelligence program, VPNs, segregated infrastructure, and dummy social media accounts are all essential tools for ensuring operational security during data collection. Organizations can effectively protect themselves from potential security breaches and cyber-attacks by implementing these measures.

Pre-configured virtual machines and other tools

Pre-configured virtual machines such as Kali Linux play a crucial role in Cyber Threat Intelligence investigations and data enrichment. These virtual machines come equipped with various tools and resources to help security professionals gather, analyze, and process information about potential cyber threats. The tools in these virtual machines are specifically designed to meet the specific needs of threat intelligence analysts and security researchers. They can be launched in any desktop virtualization software, such as VirtualBox, VMware, and others.

Kali Linux is an open-source distribution designed for penetration testing, security auditing, and other cybersecurity-related tasks. It comes pre-loaded with hundreds of tools that are ready to use, making it an ideal choice for investigators who need to launch their investigations quickly. The virtual machine is designed with a user-friendly interface, making it easy for users to navigate and utilize its tools effectively.

It is essential to note that some of the tools within Kali Linux may require third-party API keys or other configurations before they can be run effectively. Therefore, it is best to understand the tools you need to use and ensure that they are set up and ready to go before you need them.

- https://www.kali.org/get-kali/
- https://www.kali.org/tools/

For threat intelligence analysts, local applications are essential for supporting their investigations. These tools include Maltego, Recon Ng, The Harvester, Spiderfoot, and Metagoofil. They help integrate data from various sources, such as open-source intelligence (OSINT), commercial vendors, and internal sources, to establish links and correlations. They can also gather information related to domain ownership, IP address history, employee names, subdomains, open ports, and more.

In addition to local applications, security professionals can also use online tools and resources for research and investigation purposes. These include VirusTotal, URLScan, Shodan, Hybrid Analysis, and intelligenceX. These online tools provide valuable information about malware analysis, domain ownership, IP addresses, and Bitcoin addresses. However, it is crucial to understand that when using these services, the user is the product. As a result, results obtained from these services may also be available to other users, and sandboxing sensitive files may lead to a new information disclosure issue. Therefore, it is essential to review the terms and conditions of these services before using them to fully understand what will be done with the user's data.

It is worth mentioning that while these online tools and resources can be handy, it is crucial to be aware of their terms and conditions and understand what will be done with your data while using their services. Before using any of these tools, it is recommended that you review their terms and conditions to fully understand the implications of using their services.

In conclusion, pre-configured virtual machines like Kali Linux, local applications, and online tools and resources provide valuable support to Cyber Threat Intelligence investigations and data enrichment. These tools can significantly speed up gathering and analyzing data related to potential cyber threats, enabling security professionals to respond effectively and efficiently. However, using these tools with caution is essential, fully understanding their terms and conditions and implications for data privacy and security.

Where are your tools going to live?

As a cyber security professional, when building a Cyber Threat Intelligence program, it's important to consider where the tools being used for data collection will reside. The location of the tools will significantly impact their accessibility, performance, and security.

There are a few options to consider:
- **On-Premises:** Tools can be installed and run directly on the organization's servers, within their network, giving complete control and customization. However, it also requires hardware, software, licensing, maintenance, and support.

- **Cloud:** Tools can also be hosted on a cloud service, such as Amazon Web Services or Microsoft Azure, providing scalability, accessibility, and reduced IT support costs. However, it may also require increased security measures to protect sensitive data.

- **Hybrid:** A combination of on premise and cloud solutions can also be used, where specific tools are run on the premise, while others are hosted in the cloud, allowing for a tailored solution to meet specific requirements and needs.

Depending on the type of tools used and their intended purpose, it might be necessary to set them up on a segregated subnet separate from the corporate network. The reason for segregating tools used for malware or ransomware analysis from the corporate network is to prevent accidental spread to the corporate network. Setting up these tools on a dedicated system can ensure that the CTI program is not compromised. The segregated subnet can also help to minimize the risk of cyber threats and malicious attacks that could potentially infiltrate the corporate network.

When determining where your tools will live, it's important to consider factors such as:
- **Data security and privacy:** Consider the security of the data and the privacy of the information you collect and determine the best location to meet these requirements.
- **Resource constraints:** Consider the available hardware, software, and IT resources, and determine the best option based on these constraints.
- **Cost:** Evaluate the costs associated with each option and determine the most cost-effective solution for your CTI program.
- **Maintenance and support:** Consider the ongoing maintenance and support requirements for each option and determine which is the most feasible based on your resources and capabilities.

By carefully considering where the tools will reside, you can ensure that the CTI program is set up for success. Moreover, the location of the tools will determine the necessary resources and support needed for effective data collection, analysis, and response to cyber threats. It is, therefore, essential to work with IT and security teams to determine the best location for these tools, considering the resources available and the organization's overall security posture.

Overall, a successful CTI program requires an effective data collection system. By selecting the right location for the tools, you can ensure that the program is well-positioned to collect relevant and timely threat intelligence. This will ultimately lead to a more effective response to cyber threats and a more secure organizational environment.

Action items

For each intelligence requirement that has been established, determine what intelligence tools are required, as well as their dependencies to support their operationalization.

Details should include but not be limited to the following:
- Identify the intelligence sources and determine the best tools to collect information from them.
- Consider the tools needed for threat tracking, event tracking, IOCs, and course of action tracking.
- Evaluate and compare tools with similar capabilities to find the most appropriate tool to meet your requirements.
- Check if open-source or free alternatives to commercial tools exist that can perform just as well.
- Determine the compatibilities of tools (i.e., automation / integrations)

- Consider the requirements and dependencies for using and supporting the tools, such as licensing costs, hardware, software, resources, maintenance, and other support.
- Determine the setup and access for the tools and whether custom scripting can be used for additional automation and batch processing.
- Establish the operational security requirements and what is needed to support them, such as VPN services, dedicated or segregated networks, and hardware.
- Evaluate the costs of performing intelligence requirements and determine if they are cost-effective, conducting a cost-benefit analysis.
- Evaluate the costs associated with performing specific intelligence requirements and determine if they are cost-effective (risk vs. reward).
- If costs are too high vs. the potential reward, performing specific intelligence requirements may not be feasible. In this event, you have three choices:
- Drop the intelligence requirement altogether.
- Outsource the intelligence requirement to an intelligence vendor.
- Scope down the original intelligence requirement until it fits a suitable cost range while still being effective as an intelligence requirement.
- If the costs to reward is too high, consider dropping the intelligence requirement, outsourcing to an intelligence vendor, or reducing the scope of the intelligence required to fit a cost-effective range while still being effective.
- Regularly update the intelligence requirements to reflect data sources, tooling capabilities, or intelligence objectives changes.

On an ongoing basis, update the intelligence requirements to reflect any updates that have occurred as you evaluated your tools (i.e., sources may change, additional COAs because of enhanced tool capabilities, changes in the IR objective) processing (either now or in the future)

Summary

During this unit, we covered the crucial aspect of determining the right tools for the operations of the Cyber Threat Intelligence Team. This includes evaluating the cost requirements for hardware, software, and other dependencies required for various tools and intelligence needs. We also touched upon the fundamentals of operational security. We discussed the features and benefits of popular threat intelligence platforms and the pros and cons of utilizing online resources and services. Our focus was on identifying the appropriate tools for supporting and securing the CTI team, such as tracking events, courses of action, and indicators of compromise. These tools also serve as valuable data sources for reporting and metrics. With the right reporting platform, it may be possible to integrate with these tracking tools for automated reporting or real-time dashboards.

In the next unit, we will delve into reporting and establishing metrics to track the overall performance and operational improvements of the CTI team. We aim to identify areas for improvement, assess the quality of data sources, and implement process enhancements to provide a comprehensive view of the organization's internal and external threat landscape. This information can then be communicated to management to provide insight into the CTI team's efforts and outputs over a certain period.

Chapter #6 - Reporting and Metrics

Introduction

To ensure success, it is important to establish an operational metrics and reporting phase that monitors the program's activities communicates information to stakeholders and secures the necessary resources to support the program. The operational metrics and reporting phase is essential for tracking the overall effectiveness of the CTI program. It enables the CTI team to monitor the cyber threat landscape, identify emerging threats, and assess the program's response. This information is used to take appropriate action to mitigate the threats.

Regularly produced reports and metrics during this phase communicate important information to stakeholders, such as senior executives, board members, and other critical personnel. This information can include details on emerging threats, courses of action taken, operational efficiencies, and further critical details that stakeholders need to know to make informed decisions about cyber risk management.

The operational metrics and reporting phase provides visibility into the general security activities and efforts of the CTI team. By collecting and analyzing data on cyber threats and the effectiveness of the CTI program, the team can make data-driven decisions to optimize the program's performance.

In addition, regular reporting also allows the cyber threat intelligence team to:

Demonstrate value: Reporting and metrics help to demonstrate the value of the threat intelligence team's work. By quantifying the impact of the team's efforts, organizations can see the value they are getting from their investment in cyber security.

Prioritize efforts: Reporting and metrics provide valuable insights into the nature of an organization's threats, allowing teams to prioritize their efforts and focus on the most pressing issues. This helps to maximize the impact of the team's work and ensure that resources are used effectively.

Improve processes: By regularly reviewing metrics and reports, teams can identify areas for improvement in their operations and workflows. This helps to increase efficiency and effectiveness, reducing the risk of a security breach.

Measure impact: Reporting and metrics provide a way to measure the impact of the threat intelligence team's work regarding the number of threats detected and the effect of mitigation efforts. This helps organizations understand the return on their investment in cyber security and make informed decisions about future investments.

Communication: Reports and metrics clearly and concisely communicate the team's findings and activities to other departments within an organization. This helps foster better collaboration and enables different departments to take appropriate action to reduce risk.

The next step would be to secure necessary strategic direction, approval, and funding to support the CTI program, the CTI team must present a compelling business case for the program. This includes identifying the program's benefits, appropriate metrics to measure cyber threat risk and internal risk reduction and determining the required data and where to collect it.

Operational metrics and reporting	• Measure performance of the overall CTI program • Provide insight into the overall threat landscape. • Identify operational metrics and reporting to measure performance and effectiveness of the CTI team and their Courses-of-Action. • Determine required data and where to collect this.
Executive and stakeholder buy-in	• Present the business case for a Threat Intelligence Program. • Describe what a CTI Program can do for the organization. • Obtain strategic direction, approval and funding.

By presenting the business case, the CTI team can secure the necessary strategic direction, approval, and funding to support the CTI program. In conclusion, the operational metrics and reporting phase plays an essential role in the success of a CTI program by providing a framework for regularly reporting on the program's activities and performance, enabling the team to communicate important information to stakeholders, and securing the necessary resources to support the program.

The operational metrics and reporting phase is critical for the success of a CTI program. It provides a framework for regularly reporting on the program's activities and performance, communicates essential information to stakeholders, and secures the necessary resources to support the program. By leveraging this phase effectively, the CTI team can identify and mitigate cyber threats, protect the organization, and contribute to the business's overall success.

Chapter Objectives

This chapter is a crucial resource for stakeholders to understand the Cyber Threat Intelligence (CTI) program's objectives and role in an organization's security strategy. It provides comprehensive information on emerging threats being tracked by the CTI team, their mitigation strategies, and operational efficiencies achieved through the program. Stakeholders can better understand the CTI program and its vital information.

Upon completion of this chapter, participants will be able to:
- Establish reporting cadence and criteria for executives and stakeholders.
- Formulate meaningful operational metrics to be included in various reporting products.
- Prepare reporting templates and layouts based on reporting requirements and audience.
- Construct methods to acquire and generate updated data and metrics efficiently.

Operational Metrics

CTI teams collect and track data during regular operations and store it in various intelligence platforms to better understand the threat landscape. Using metrics helps CTI teams track their performance over time, identify trends and patterns in the threat landscape, and inform future strategies and tactics. However, not all metrics are created equal. A well-designed metric is meaningful, easily calculated, and acquired, providing insight into the specific threat landscape. A poorly designed metric can be of little value, such as a simple count of Indicators of Compromise (IOCs) added to the Security Information and Event Management (SIEM) system, as it needs more insight into the specifics of the threat landscape.

To gain a more granular representation of the threat landscape, the CTI team can cross-tabulate metrics with other data points, such as IOCs related to critical and zero-day exploitation of technologies used within the organization. Key Performance Indicators (KPIs) and Key Risk Indicators (KRIs) are two crucial operational metrics for the CTI team. KPIs provide quantifiable performance measurements over time, measuring historical performance, while KRIs give an early signal of increasing risk to an organization, offering a forward-looking view.

- **Key Performance Indicators (KPIs):** A quantifiable performance measurement over time for a specific Intelligence Requirement (historical).

- **Key Risk Indicators (KRIs):** KRIs provide an early signal of increasing risk towards the organization (forward view).

It is important to note that using operational metrics and reporting is crucial for the CTI team and plays a significant role in helping stakeholders make informed decisions. The CTI team can use the metrics and reports to provide necessary information to stakeholders, including senior management, to make informed decisions on the organization's security posture.

Operational metrics and reporting are critical for the success of a Cyber Threat Intelligence team. By implementing well-designed metrics and regularly tracking them, the CTI team can effectively measure its performance and understand the cyber threat landscape, identify trends, and inform future strategies and tactics. Additionally, by using KPIs and KRIs, the CTI team can make informed decisions and provide stakeholders with the necessary information to make informed decisions.

Threat Landscape

By leveraging threat landscape metrics, organizations can prioritize their defense efforts and allocate resources effectively to mitigate potential security risks. Making informed decisions about deploying security technologies and tactics is vital in today's ever-changing threat landscape. Organizations that can stay ahead of the curve and anticipate emerging threats are better equipped to prevent security incidents before they occur.

Threat landscape metrics provide a high-level overview of emerging threats that may impact an organization, sector, industry, or global landscape. By tracking and trending metadata associated with these threats, such as location, type of threat, industry, or specific vulnerabilities, organizations can gain a clear view of the threat landscape and potentially upcoming threats or risks that may be observed in the future.

Sample Metrics include but are not limited to:
- Most prominent emerging cyber threats
- Ransomware/malware variants
- Threat group activity (frequency, targets/victims)
- Actively exploited vulnerabilities and software applications
- Threats targeting specific sectors, industries, and region.

Data Source: The information source for these metrics is typically derived from daily monitoring of media sources, community newsgroups, trusted third parties, and other relevant and supporting sources.

The value to the overall organization in having the cyber threat intelligence team track these metrics allows for understanding and interpreting the following:
- **Trend Analysis:** Threat landscape metrics allow organizations to track and analyze trends in emerging threats over time. This information helps organizations understand the nature and scope of the threat environment and predict future trends, allowing them to prepare for potential threats and respond proactively.

- **Resource Allocation:** Threat landscape metrics provide valuable information about the distribution of threats across industries, regions, and other demographics. This information can help organizations allocate resources effectively, ensuring that the areas with the most significant risk receive the necessary attention and resources.

- **Threat Prioritization:** Threat landscape metrics clearly understand the current threat environment, allowing organizations to prioritize their defense efforts. This information helps organizations identify the most critical threats and allocate resources accordingly, allowing them to respond proactively to the most severe threats.

- **Threat Characterization:** Threat landscape metrics provide information about the nature of emerging threats, including the type of attack, target, and motivation. This information helps organizations understand the motivations behind attacks, allowing them to respond more effectively and take proactive steps to prevent similar attacks in the future.

Tracking and analyzing trends in the threat environment can help organizations respond proactively, as opposed to being reactive after an incident has occurred. This proactive approach enables organizations to be better prepared to defend against emerging threats and reduces the overall impact of security incidents on their operations.

Threat landscape metrics are a critical component of a robust CTI program. By providing valuable information about emerging threats and allowing organizations to respond proactively, these metrics enable organizations to prioritize their defense efforts, allocate resources effectively, and make informed decisions about deploying security technologies and tactics. By staying ahead of the curve, organizations can better protect their operations, customers, and reputation in the face of evolving cyber threats.

Detection Stemming from CTI

Measuring the effectiveness of a Cyber Threat Intelligence (CTI) program is crucial for organizations to prioritize and allocate resources, demonstrate return on investment (ROI), and support compliance efforts. The "Detection Stemming from CTI" metric provides valuable insights into the quality of threat intelligence indicators, the subsequent investigation results, and the performance of security appliances and systems.

This metric is based on the activity of security information and event management (SIEM) systems and other security appliances, as well as the quality of threat feed sources and existing detection rules. By measuring the number of alerts triggered within the SIEM or other security appliances based on the implemented detection rules and indicators of compromise (IOCs), organizations can gain valuable insights into the quality of their threat intelligence indicators and the performance of their security controls.

In addition to the number of alerts triggered, this metric also provides information about the types and sources of indicators, as well as threat categories and classifications. This information helps organizations validate the quality of their indicator sources and make informed decisions about future investments in CTI.

Metrics: Measure of alerts triggered within the SIEM, or other security appliances based on the implemented detection rules and/or IOCs:
- Total Detections (True / False Positives)
- Detections blocked because of an existing security control.
- Indicator type (domain, URL, file hash, IP)
- Indicator source (commercial, OSINT, internal, etc.)
- Threat category / classification

Data Source: Multiple data sources will be used to calculate these metrics, including various SOC management and ticketing system (used to track events and incidents), the SIEM, other security appliances, threat intelligence platform, and other data repositories.

The value to the overall organization in having the cyber threat intelligence team track these metrics allows for understanding and interpreting the following:
- **Effectiveness:** Metrics and tracking help organizations understand the effectiveness of their CTI program by measuring the number of threats detected, the time it takes to detect and respond to threats, and the impact of threats on the organization. For example, tracking the number of successful attacks and incidents prevented by the CTI program can provide valuable insights into the program's effectiveness.

- **Prioritization:** By tracking the types of threats facing the organization and their frequency, organizations can prioritize their efforts to address the most critical risks. For example, tracking the number of phishing attacks and the number of successful breaches can help organizations prioritize their efforts to mitigate these types of threats.

- **Resource allocation:** Metrics can help organizations allocate resources effectively by demonstrating where resources are most needed. For example, tracking the number of successful attacks from a specific geographic location can help organizations allocate resources to defend against these threats.

- **Return on Investment (ROI):** CTI metrics provide data-driven evidence of the return on investment in the CTI program. By tracking the program's costs and comparing them to the benefits, organizations can determine the financial recovery they are getting from their investment in CTI. This information can be used to justify future program investments and ensure that the program remains a priority for the organization.

- **Compliance:** In regulated industries, tracking and reporting on CTI metrics can help demonstrate compliance with regulations and standards. For example, in the healthcare industry, organizations must comply with the Health Insurance Portability and Accountability Act (HIPAA), which requires protecting patient data. By tracking and reporting on CTI metrics, organizations can demonstrate their commitment to protecting patient data and ensuring compliance with HIPAA regulations.

To calculate these metrics, leverage multiple data sources such as incident and event management systems, SIEM systems, and threat intelligence platforms are used. By tracking these metrics over time, organizations can gain a better understanding of the effectiveness of their CTI program and make necessary adjustments to improve their security posture. Overall, in tracking "Detection Stemming from CTI" is important as it provides valuable insights into the quality of threat intelligence indicators, the performance of security controls and systems, and helps organizations make informed decisions about resource allocation and future investments in CTI.

Performance of CTI Vendors, Internal Tools and Data sources

Performance metrics for CTI Vendors, Internal Tools, and Data Sources are used to measure their performance and effectiveness in providing valuable and accurate threat intelligence. These metrics provide insight into the uptime performance and quality of the CTI vendors and internal tools and the intelligence sources they rely on. By measuring various performance metrics, the CTI team can better understand the strengths and weaknesses of the vendors, tools, and data sources they use to gather threat intelligence. This information can then be used to make informed decisions about improving the CTI program, including choosing new or different tools, adjusting the use of existing tools, or adjusting the sources of intelligence used.

For example, suppose the CTI team determines that a particular tool or source consistently provides low-quality or unreliable intelligence. In that case, they may decide to discontinue the use of that tool or source and seek alternative options. On the other hand, if a tool or source is consistently providing high-quality and reliable intelligence, the CTI team may choose to increase their use of that tool or source.

Metric:
- CTI Vendor Product SLAs (SLA compliance vs. non-compliant):
  - Vendor Services and internal tooling Uptime / SLAs (associated internal / external tools, services, intel sources, web portals, IOC feed servers)
  - Operational Impacts (Effort and resources to resolve technical issues or tool/service downtime (Human resources, financial cost))
- Intel/data source frequency and Confidence:
  - What is the quality and confidence of intel and data you are receiving from your intel/data sources
  - How often do you receive intel from your various data sources
  - What is the intel source True/False positive rate

Data Source: Service owners will be responsible for tracking the downtime of various intelligence tools. When a service tool is required yet unavailable, this impacts the performance of the CTI. The CTI Team may request details regarding these downtimes.

The value to the overall organization in having the cyber threat intelligence team track these metrics allows for understanding and interpreting the following:

- **Performance Metrics:** Performance metrics, such as the number of threats detected, the accuracy of threat intelligence, and time to detection, can be used to assess the effectiveness of CTI services and sources. By tracking these metrics over time, the CTI team can identify areas where a particular service or source is performing well and where improvements are needed.

- **Feedback Loops:** Feedback from stakeholders, such as security operations teams or incident responders, can provide insight into the usefulness and relevance of the CTI services and sources. The CTI team can use this feedback to adjust their services and sources, ensuring they are providing the right intelligence at the right time.

- **Intel Data Source Frequency and Confidence:** Regular assessments of the quality and confidence of the intelligence data received from various intelligence sources. The frequency of intelligence data obtained from these sources and the true positive/false positive rate of these sources can inform the CTI team on the effectiveness of these sources. By addressing these issues, the CTI team can ensure that they provide stakeholders with high-quality, actionable intelligence.

- **Service Level Agreements (SLAs):** This is a measurement of compliance versus non-compliance with the service level agreements between the CTI team and the vendors providing the CTI services and sources. This assesses the uptime performance and quality of the CTI vendors and tools.

- **Tooling Uptime:** This measures the uptime performance of internal and external CTI tools, services, intelligence sources, web portals, Indicator of Compromise (IOC) feed servers, etc. Downtime of CTI tools and services can impact the performance of the CTI team by taking away resources that could be spent on analyst activities.

- **Efforts and Resources to Resolve Technical Issues:** Technical difficulties with CTI tools and services can result in a human resource cost and a financial cost to resolve the issues. The CTI team is responsible for tracking and resolving these technical issues, which can impact their overall performance.

Tracking the performance metrics of your vendors, tools, and data sources are essential to a successful CTI team. In assessing their effectiveness, it is possible to identify areas for improvement and make informed decisions about improving the CTI program. By doing so, the CTI team can ensure that the intelligence gathered is of the highest quality and that the CTI program is operating efficiently and effectively.

Security Enhancements as a result of CTI

The significance of Cyber Threat Intelligence (CTI) in enhancing an organization's security posture must be considered. The CTI team regularly identifies emerging cyber threats and determines the courses of action to take to defend against these threats. Using metrics in CTI enables assessing the efficiency of these action plans and identifying areas that require improvement.

The CTI team's efforts involve various courses of action, including detect, discover, disrupt, degrade, deceive, and destroy. By tracking the effectiveness of these strategies, the team can identify the most successful tactics for combating emerging cyber threats. This not only highlights the team's strengths but also allows them to focus on the most efficient courses of action. The data collected from these metrics can be obtained from multiple tracking systems and assist in providing recommendations to other teams to improve the organization's security posture.

Using metrics helps to identify the most effective courses of action by classification. This highlights the CTI team's strengths and allows them to concentrate on the most successful strategies for combating emerging cyber threats. The data for these metrics can be obtained from multiple tracking systems, and these metrics assist in providing recommendations to other teams to enhance the security posture of the entire organization.

Metric:
- Count COAs by Classification (Discover, Detect, Deny, Disrupt, Degrade, Deceive, Destroy)
- Most commonly implemented CoA by Classification (i.e. Top 3):
  - Highlights capabilities of the CTI team and where improvements can be made
  - Most commonly leveraged security appliance/tool (i.e. IDS/IPS, Firewall Detection Signatures (Yara, Snort, etc…))
- Recommendations to other teams:
  - IT and Desktop Services / application development (i.e., settings and configuration recommendations (non-indicator based)
  - Vulnerability Management (i.e., System Patching)

- Most effective COAs by classification (i.e., Top 3):
  - Highlights strengths of the CTI Team and where improvements can be made.

Data Source: These metrics will be derived from your COAs tracking system. Suppose multiple teams are using various tracking systems. In that case, you may have to derive data from other problem management and ticketing systems where tracking activities may have occurred from other teams involved in CTI.

The value to the overall organization in having the cyber threat intelligence team track these metrics allows for understanding and interpreting the following:

- **Improved security posture:** Implementing security enhancements due to cyber threat intelligence allows organizations to improve their security posture. This includes strengthening the defense against emerging cyber threats, protecting sensitive information and assets, and reducing the risk of cyber-attacks. Using metrics in cyber threat intelligence helps organizations identify areas for improvement and implement strategies to enhance their security posture.

- **Data-driven decision-making:** By using metrics to measure the effectiveness of their courses of action, organizations can make informed decisions about their security strategies based on data and evidence. This enables organizations to make informed decisions about their security posture and allocate resources efficiently.

- **Increased efficiency:** Using metrics in cyber threat intelligence helps organizations track the most effective courses of action and identify areas for improvement. This allows organizations to streamline their security efforts and allocate resources more efficiently. By focusing on the most effective strategies, organizations can maximize the impact of their security enhancements and minimize waste.
- **Proactive threat defense:** The ability to identify emerging threats and implement appropriate courses of action allows organizations to take a proactive approach to threat defense. This helps prevent potential attacks before they occur rather than responding to attacks after they have occurred. With metrics, organizations can track the effectiveness of their courses of action and make improvements as needed to stay ahead of emerging threats.

By implementing security enhancements and tracking metrics, the CTI team can support the organization in improving its overall security posture, making informed decisions based on data and evidence, streamlining its security efforts, and taking a proactive approach to threat defense. Organizations can use cyber threat intelligence to protect their assets and sensitive information from emerging cyber threats and maintain a solid and effective defense against cyber-attacks.

CTI Products and Services

By tracking relevant metrics, the CTI team can gain a deeper understanding of the strengths and weaknesses of each intelligence requirement and associated product and service, which helps identify areas for improvement. This is crucial for preventing emerging cyber threats and ensuring that the organization remains secure.

Metrics related to CTI Products and Services performance can provide valuable information for the annual evaluations of the CTI program. These metrics can help determine which intelligence requirements, products, and services are helpful, which need improvement, and which require better sources or enhancements to improve delivery methods and service level agreements. By analyzing these metrics, the CTI team can ensure that the CTI program effectively defends the organization against cyber threats.

Metric:
- Which intelligence requirements are most often triggered or actioned?
- Which Intel products and services are the most effective in defending the organization against cyber-threats
- What Intel Requirements, Products and Services are time consuming and yield little value
- How can Intel products and services be enhanced to improve their effectiveness and or delivery of SLA.
- Do gaps exist in collection sources, current capabilities, or require manual intervention (manual efforts vs. automated)
- How many intelligence products have been produced?
- Has feedback from stakeholders regarding CTI intel products and services been positive or negative.

Data Source: This information used to support these metrics is derived from internal CTI data repositories, including COA and IOC tracking systems and other ticket management systems. Additional supporting information can be obtained through stakeholder/recipient feedback.

The value to the overall organization in having the cyber threat intelligence team track these metrics allows for understanding and interpreting the following:

- **Evaluation of Effectiveness:** Metrics help to assess the effectiveness of the products and services in detecting, preventing, and responding to cyber threats. This allows organizations to identify gaps in their threat intelligence capabilities and make necessary improvements.

- **Better Decision-Making:** Metrics provide the data required for evidence-based decision-making, which helps organizations to prioritize their cyber security investments and allocate resources more effectively.

- **Continuously Evaluate and Improve Capabilities:** By regularly tracking and producing metrics on the products and services used for threat intelligence, organizations can identify areas for improvement and make necessary changes. This can help organizations continuously optimize their threat intelligence capabilities, stay ahead of evolving threats, and reduce the risk of successful cyber-attacks.

- **Improved Planning:** Metrics help organizations to plan their intelligence-gathering activities more effectively and allocate resources more efficiently.

Tracking and producing metrics on the performance and evaluation of your CTI products and services enables the team to continuously evaluate and improve their capabilities, prioritize their efforts, and demonstrate the value of their activities to stakeholders. This ultimately enhances the organization's overall security posture by allowing them to defend against and prevent cyber-attacks.

Reporting

Generating and sharing reports is an essential part of the CTI Team. However, it's important to understand that each type of report has its purpose, audience, frequency, and format. As a result, the CTI team must align these elements to ensure that the reports are both meaningful and effective.

The primary purpose of any report is to communicate information, so the report's intent should be clearly defined. It could be to communicate the current threat landscape, track trends and progress, ensure accountability, or facilitate continuous improvement. Therefore, the message cadence should also be carefully considered, with reports being produced at the appropriate frequency to support the intent of the report.

To ensure that reports are produced efficiently and effectively, the CTI team should take advantage of existing CTI tools to streamline the appropriate data acquisition. This would not only reduce the time spent collecting information but also ensure that the information provided is accurate and up to date. Using templates to standardize the report's format would also ensure consistency in the reporting process and incorporate the corporate brand into the report.

It's important to strike a balance between the amount of reporting needed and each report's content. Generating reports requires time and effort from one or more resources, so reports should not be produced simply for the sake of generating a report. If a report does not provide meaningful information to stakeholders, then the report should be discontinued or repurposed.

Daily Reports

The daily threat intelligence report typically includes a summary of the most significant and relevant information that the organization needs to be aware of, such as newly discovered vulnerabilities, malware, phishing attacks, or any other significant threat that could impact the organization. It may also include recommendations and advice on how to mitigate the risks and protect against potential threats.

The report provides a summary of information collected from a variety of sources, including:
- Security blogs and forums
- Social media platforms
- News articles
- Reports from security vendors
- Dark web sources

Daily reporting is recommended as this is used to collect threat-related information that helps to establish the following:
- Threat landscape
- Commonly targeted regions
- Commonly targeted sectors and industries
- Information on widely used Tactics, Techniques, & Procedures (TTPs).
- The report typically includes:
- A severity rating.
- Attack vector information.
- Associated Common Vulnerabilities and Exposures (CVEs).
- An assessment of the risk and impact on the organization.

This information can help organizations to prioritize their defense efforts and to develop a strategy to mitigate potential threats. The report is usually delivered via email to critical members of the organization's privacy, security, and IT teams.

Daily Threat Intelligence Brief – March 13th, 2019

Analyst: Robert Vidal

Wednesday March 13th, 2019

Third-Party Online Chat Service Responsible for Data Breach Affecting Best Buy, Delta Airlines and Sears Holdings

Severity: HIGH

Attack Vector: Supply Chain Attack

Details:

- The breach occurred between September 26th, and October 12th, of 2017, when malware infected the systems of [24]7.ai, an online chat service.
- It is believed the threat actor gained access to payment card numbers, CVVs, and expiration dates, as well as names and addresses of those compromised. A Delta spokesperson stated that less than 100,000 customers were affected, yet hundreds of thousands more could potentially be exposed.
- The malware was removed on October 12th, 2017 and [24]7.ai spent five and a half months investigating the incident together with law enforcement.

Risk and Impact: With this information it is possible for threat actors to use the compromised data for financial fraud against the victims.

Recommendations: It is recommended that organizations have processes and procedures in place to assess security risks and concerns related to the integration of third party tools used within public facing applications. In addition, Incident Handling Procedures should be in place and ready in the event of an incident to prevent prolonged investigations.

Associated CVEs: 2018-2385

Courses of Action:

- Vulnerability Management notified of the vulnerable CVE and advised the associated patch was applied during the previous patch cycle.
- IOCs obtained and searched within the SIEM with no detections discovered.
- IOCs added to ongoing monitoring.

References: Bleeping Computers

The report provides recommendations for organizations to defend against cyber threats, including implementing software patches, enhancing employee security awareness, and adopting new security technologies. It aims to equip organizations with the necessary information to proactively defend against threats and quickly respond to security incidents if they occur.

To ensure that teams are equipped with the latest information at the start of their day, the Daily Threat Report should be sent out early to mid-morning. It should be customized to the specific needs and concerns of the organization and its industry, providing a quick and concise summary of critical information about emerging threats.

Format: Email sent to Distribution List.
SLAs: 10 am Daily
Intended Audience: A daily report is intended for general employees within Privacy, Security, and IT Teams.

Weekly Reporting

A weekly threat intelligence report is an essential tool that provides critical information about emerging and ongoing cyber security threats, risks, and vulnerabilities. This report is typically prepared by a team of expert cyber security professionals or specialized threat intelligence companies, and it is distributed to organizations, governments, and individuals who are interested in staying informed about the current cyber threat landscape.

The report encompasses different aspects of cyber security, such as identifying new and ongoing phishing campaigns, malware and ransomware attacks, data breaches, and vulnerabilities in various software, hardware, or networking products. Moreover, the report includes recommendations on how organizations can safeguard themselves from the identified threats and mitigate associated risks.

Weekly reports also contain some high-level metrics related to:
- Top threats for the week
- Threat and other notable events

- Top detections
- Summary of COAs

The purpose of a weekly threat intelligence report is to provide organizations with timely and relevant information about the cyber security landscape. This information helps organizations make informed decisions about their cyber security posture and take proactive steps to defend against potential attacks. In today's ever-evolving threat landscape, a weekly threat intelligence report is critical for keeping organizations informed and prepared.

Typically, a weekly threat intelligence report is a one or two-page document, often delivered in PDF format. It contains executive-level summaries of the threat events that have been identified, as well as the actions taken by the Cyber Threat Intelligence (CTI) team to address these threats. The report also provides high-level metrics related to the top threats for the week and notable events. This makes it an easily digestible resource for IT and security personnel at the management level.

The CTI team delivers the weekly report a few days after the previous week, with service level agreements set for Tuesday of the following week. This allows organizations to stay informed about the latest threats and take appropriate measures to protect their networks and data promptly. In short, a weekly threat intelligence report is an indispensable tool for organizations looking to maintain a proactive stance against cyber security threats.

Format: A weekly report is typically 1-2 pages long in word format and delivered as a PDF to appropriate stakeholders.
SLAs: Tuesday of the following week
Intended Audience: The weekly report is intended for management-level members of the Privacy, Security, and IT Teams.

Monthly

The monthly threat intelligence report is a comprehensive document that offers organizations valuable insights into the current threat landscape. It overviews prevalent threats, most exploited vulnerabilities, and high and critical severity threat detections. The report's ThreatCon overview offers an in-depth analysis of the organization, industry, or global threat landscape, enabling organizations to comprehend the current cybersecurity threat scenario and make informed decisions to safeguard their systems and data.

The report includes a detailed analysis of metrics and trends related to the threat landscape. It highlights widespread threats and trends, most exploited CVEs (Common Vulnerabilities and Exposures), and metrics associated with high and critical severity threat detections. By comparing these metrics month over month, organizations can evaluate the current state of the threat landscape and identify areas of concern that may necessitate additional security measures.

Monthly reports contain some detailed metrics and trends related to:
- ThreatCon Overview (Organization, Industry, Global)
- Threat Landscape:
- Popular threats and trends
- Most exploited CVE
- High and critical severity threats detections
- The CTI team took Courses-of-Action to help defend against identified threats.
- Monthly CTI operational metrics

The report also provides information on the steps taken by the CTI team to defend against identified threats. This information includes measures to mitigate threats, such as applying security patches, deploying firewalls, and updating antivirus software. Organizations can use this information to evaluate the effectiveness of their existing security measures and identify areas where they need to enhance their security posture.

In addition to threat-related information, the monthly report includes operational metrics related to CTI activities. These metrics include the number of security incidents detected, response time, and the efficacy of the current security measures. These metrics provide a comprehensive view of the security operations' performance and help organizations identify areas for improvement.

Format: A monthly report is typically 6-8 PowerPoint slides delivered as a PDF to appropriate stakeholders.
SLAs: 10 business days into the following month
Intended Audience: The monthly report is intended for upper management-level members of the Privacy, Security, and IT Teams.

Quarterly Reports

Organizations rely on the quarterly threat intelligence report as an indispensable resource to gain a comprehensive understanding of the current threat landscape and the measures undertaken by the CTI team to bolster the overall security posture. This report covers the preceding three months and presents the latest information on the prevailing cyber security scenario, keeping stakeholders informed and up to date.

The report furnishes vital data and metrics related to the current threat landscape, including significant geopolitical and socio-economic events that may pose security risks to the organization. It also provides insights into the common Tactics, Techniques, and Procedures (TTPs) used by cyber criminals, noteworthy industry events, and the actions taken by the CTI team to augment the organization's security posture. By comparing these metrics to the previous quarters, the report helps identify trends in the threat landscape and CTI operations, enabling proactive measures to counter potential risks.

Quarterly reports contain some detailed metrics and trends related to:
- Current Threat Condition (Major Global Geopolitical and Socio-Economical Events)
- Threat Landscape trends (i.e., threat types, targeted Regions/industries)
- Threat Trends on commonly used TTPs
- Notable Industry Events
- The CTI team took COAs to enhance the organization's overall security posture.

The format of the quarterly threat intelligence report may vary, but it is typically presented as a slide deck or a word document that contains detailed information and writing. While the length of the report may vary, it should be comprehensive enough to provide a complete and accurate portrayal of the threat landscape and the measures undertaken by the CTI team to strengthen the organization's security posture.

The primary audience for the quarterly report is typically board-level members of the organization, and it is usually delivered one month after the end of the quarter. The report provides a comprehensive overview of the current threat landscape and the measures taken by the CTI team to bolster the organization's security posture. This allows stakeholders to make well-informed decisions regarding cyber security.

The quarterly threat intelligence report serves as a crucial tool for organizations to comprehend the current threat landscape and take proactive steps to improve their overall security posture. It furnishes stakeholders with the requisite information and data to make sound decisions related to cyber security.

Format: A quarterly report could be produced as a slide deck or Word document, depending on stakeholders' requirements.
SLAs: 1 month after the quarter
Intended Audience: The quarterly report is intended for Board level members of the organization.

Annual Reports

The annual threat intelligence report serves as a critical resource for organizations to gain a holistic understanding of the current threat landscape and its potential impact on their security posture. This report delivers a comprehensive overview of the various types of threats, significant events, and trends observed over the past year. Furthermore, it provides a detailed analysis of the CTI team's strategic approach to strengthen the organization's security posture and mitigate potential risks, thus ensuring that the organization is adequately prepared to tackle emerging cyber threats.

Annual Reports are used to:

- Threat landscape events and trends observed over the past year
- Describes COAs taken by the CTI team to enhance the security posture of the organization.
- Provide details regarding operational insight and effectiveness (i.e., intelligence sources, Intelligence Requirements)

The report provides essential information on the CTI team's intelligence sources and requirements, including a comprehensive analysis of the data sources utilized to collect and assess threat information. This information is critical to enable upper management and board-level members to make informed decisions regarding the organization's security strategy and resource allocation. The report allows decision-makers to understand the threat landscape more thoroughly and evaluate the CTI team's ability to provide accurate, timely, and relevant intelligence. By utilizing this information, organizations can take proactive steps to enhance their security posture and safeguard against potential cyber threats.

This report provides top-level decision-makers with the information needed to:

- Provide strategic direction and corporate insight to prioritize efforts.
- Consider the following year's budget and resources.
- Annual reports could take a significant amount of time to produce and should have an SLA of up to 3 months.

The production of the annual threat intelligence report is a time-consuming process, with a service level agreement of up to three months after the first quarter. The report is typically created in a user-friendly Word format that includes a large amount of content and storytelling. The report is intended for upper management and board-level members of the organization and is several hundred pages long.

This report is a critical resource for organizations, providing valuable insights into current cyber threats and their potential impact. It helps inform security strategies and resource allocation decisions while also providing operational insights into the effectiveness of the CTI team. Overall, the annual threat intelligence report is essential for any organization looking to maintain a proactive and effective cybersecurity posture.

Format: Annual reports are relatively long and produced as a slide deck or Word document, depending on stakeholders' requirements.
SLAs: Before the end of the following Q1
Intended Audience: The annual report is intended for upper management and board members.

Action Items

From the Intelligence products and services that were established in previous chapters, identify and document the reporting requirements, formats, and cadence for each stakeholder, team, and or other audience:

- This is dependent on stakeholder requirements.
- Identify the distribution and audience for each product.
- The ideal would be daily, monthly, quarterly, annual, and ad-hoc reports (i.e., Flash notifications, Intelligence Briefings, etc...)
- Identify meaningful metrics:
    o Proactively identified threats that could impact the organization.
    o COAs were taken to enhance the overall security posture.
    o Mitigations implemented to defend against emerging threats.
- Mock-up potential reporting templates:
    o Determine how metric data will be obtained and generated.
    o Determine where other content will be derived.
    o Other information as necessary

Summary

In this chapter, we delved into the importance of establishing a robust reporting and metrics system for the cyber threat intelligence (CTI) team. The goal was to provide stakeholders and executives with meaningful insights into the efficiency and effectiveness of the CTI team and to help them make informed decisions about the team's activities and resource allocation.

We discussed formulating operational metrics to be included in various reporting products to achieve this. This included identifying key performance indicators that accurately reflect the team's performance and measuring the impact of the team's activities on the organization's security posture. We also covered preparing reporting templates and layouts based on reporting requirements and audience, ensuring that the reports are concise, well-structured, and easy to understand for stakeholders. Additionally, we discussed the importance of constructing methods to quickly acquire and generate updated data and metrics to keep the reporting products current and relevant.

The next chapter will focus on presenting the vision of the CTI team to executives and stakeholders for approval. The goal is to obtain dedicated resources, including budget, technical, and human resources, to stand up and operate a CTI service and to obtain executive authorization to utilize these resources. Additionally, the reporting requirements and cadence must be established so stakeholders and executives can track the team's progress and make informed decisions. This chapter emphasized the critical role of reporting and metrics in the success of a CTI program and laid the foundation for obtaining executive and stakeholder buy-in.

Chapter #7 - Executive and Stakeholder Buy-in

Introduction

To comprehensively understand the importance of obtaining executive and stakeholder buy-in, it is important to consider the various challenges that organizations face in building and maintaining a successful cyber threat intelligence program. For example, without the support of executives and stakeholders, the necessary resources and funding for the program may not be allocated, and the program may not align with the overall goals and objectives of the organization. With all stakeholders' buy-in, a cybersecurity awareness culture may be cultivated. This lack of awareness can result in a lack of understanding about the importance of the program and the critical role it plays in protecting the organization from cyber threats. This, in turn, can result in a lack of support for the program and its goals, which can be detrimental to its success.

Organizations must understand the importance of obtaining executive and stakeholder buy-in when building a cyber threat intelligence program and operations. This not only helps to ensure the necessary resources and funding are allocated, but it also fosters a culture of cybersecurity awareness and aligns the program with the organization's goals and objectives. By doing so, organizations can better tackle the ever-evolving cyber threat landscape and protect themselves from cyber-attacks.

Executive and stakeholder buy-in	• Present the business case for a Threat Intelligence Program. • Describe what a CTI Program can do for the organization. • Obtain strategic direction, approval and funding.
CTI Setup and on-going operations	• Implement the tools and processes that have been established to monitor your intelligence requirements.

This chapter aims to obtain approval and funding before procuring resources to support the CTI program. The presentation will include the business case for the CTI program, what it can do for the organization, and the strategic direction. Once executive and stakeholder approval is obtained, the next step is to set up ongoing operations for the CTI program, which includes implementing tools and processes to monitor and action upon your intelligence requirements.

Chapter Objectives:

This chapter focuses on leveraging all the previous chapters and work efforts that you have performed to demonstrate your plan for a CTI program to your executives and stakeholders.

Upon completion of this chapter, participants will be able to:
- Develop executive and stakeholder presentations regarding the Intelligence Requirements and CTI operations that have been established to obtain support and buy-in.
- Justify identified cyber threats and their associated Intelligence Requirement proposals on identifying and defending against them.

- Appraise, tailor, and update Intelligence Requirements based on executive and stakeholder feedback.

What can CTI do for an organization

The CTI program is designed to proactively monitor identified intelligence requirements, reducing the organization's exposure to cyber threats. This results in minimizing operational downtime during a cyber-attack, reducing incident and recovery costs, and preventing reputational damage. Additionally, the CTI program enhances the organization's security posture by identifying emerging cyber threats and providing recommendations for improving security monitoring and controls.

To effectively communicate the benefits of the CTI program to executives and stakeholders, it is crucial to present the potential risks the organization may face without a CTI program and how the CTI program can mitigate those risks. This can be achieved by introducing the program's objectives, services, and products and how they align with the organization's risk mitigation strategies. Any concerns or objections from executives and stakeholders should also be addressed to demonstrate the value the CTI program will bring to the organization.

The key to gaining executive and stakeholder buy-in is to provide a clear and concise proposal for the new CTI program, outlining how it will mitigate cyber risks for the organization. This includes identifying intelligence requirements, reducing exposure to cyber threats, and understanding threat actors, their motives, and attack techniques. By reducing operational downtime and recovery costs, preventing reputational impacts, and enhancing the organization's security posture, the CTI program will support the organization's risk mitigation strategies.

By demonstrating the value of the CTI program and addressing any concerns or objections from executives and stakeholders, the CTI team can ensure the necessary support and commitments from the organization. This will enable the CTI program to achieve its objectives, mitigate cyber risks, and provide real value to the organization. In conclusion, a well-communicated and well-supported CTI program can be a significant asset to an organization's cyber security posture.

What threats can the CTI Team defend against

In the third chapter of this book, we conducted Threat Modeling activities to identify potential cyber threats that could impact the organization and its operations. The threat models developed in this chapter are crucial as they serve as a foundation to establish Intelligence Requirements. By mapping the threats to specific Intelligence Requirements, we can identify the assets, technologies, and lines of business that require protection from potential cyber threats. This process ensures that executives and stakeholders understand the need to safeguard these areas.

After identifying potential cyber threats, the CTI team can establish Intelligence Requirements to monitor and respond to. These Intelligence Requirements provide a comprehensive outline of the CTI products, services, and courses of action that the team will take to defend against identified cyber threats. To maximize the effectiveness of the intelligence requirements, they should align with the organization's security strategy and direction and be actionable to provide the most value.

The intelligence requirements complement the organization's existing capabilities and make it easier to implement recommended security measures. By presenting these requirements, the CTI team outlines its steps to defend against potential cyber threats. This level of detail and proactive approach to cybersecurity demonstrates the team's expertise and competence and provides a sense of security to executives and stakeholders.

What Courses-of-Action (COAs), Products and Services will be produced

Effective communication of intelligence requirements and plans to executives and stakeholders is critical. It is necessary to highlight specific courses of action, products, and services employed to safeguard the organization against identified threats and deliver the most significant value.

Clear and concise explanations of the products and services will help ensure that everyone understands the benefits of your efforts. For instance, it is important to explain the measures that will be taken to monitor emerging threats such as malware and ransomware, such as implementing security measures to prevent communication with malicious actors by utilizing file hashes, IP addresses, domains, and URLs. It is also crucial to emphasize close collaboration with the vulnerability management team to identify and eliminate any vulnerable or exploited technologies in the environment.

By providing precise and concise explanations of the courses of action, products, and services that will be implemented, you can ensure that everyone comprehends the benefits of your efforts and the value that will be delivered to the organization. This approach promotes transparency and fosters a culture of trust that can help establish strong relationships between your team, executives, and stakeholders.

Organizational Support for the CTI Program

When seeking support from executives and stakeholders, provide a clear understanding of the resources required to establish and sustain the CTI team. This includes financial support for hiring talented cybersecurity professionals and acquiring necessary tools and technologies. The organization must also provide dedicated facilities for the CTI team to operate effectively, ensuring they have the essential tools, equipment, and environment to carry out their duties.

Be sure to highlight the need for organizational support to foster collaboration between the CTI team and other IT teams. This includes encouraging other IT teams to work closely with the CTI team and promote a culture of information sharing and cooperation. By establishing a culture of collaboration, the CTI team can effectively share information and resources, identify common goals, and enhance the organization's overall security posture.

The role of executives and stakeholders in providing the CTI (Cyber Threat Intelligence) team with adequate resources and support cannot be overstated. With their permission, the CTI team may be able to effectively carry out its duties and protect the organization against cyber threats. However, with the right resources and support, the CTI team can operate at optimal capacity and play a crucial role in securing the organization. Hence, securing executive and stakeholder support is vital for the CTI team's success and the organization's overall security.

Human Capital

A CTI program is critical to an organization's overall cybersecurity strategy. It provides valuable information about the latest threats, trends, and adversary tactics, techniques, and procedures (TTPs), allowing organizations to stay ahead of potential attacks. However, to effectively implement and run a CTI program, a team of skilled individuals must be dedicated to the task.

The CTI team ensures that the CTI program is aligned with the organization's intelligence requirements and executes the various CTI operations effectively. To be successful, the team must have a clear understanding of the intelligence requirements and have access to the necessary resources and tools. This includes technical equipment, software and databases, and other essential resources required to carry out the various CTI operations, such as data collection, analysis, and dissemination.

The size and composition of the CTI team will depend on the scope of the CTI program and the specific intelligence requirements of the organization. In smaller organizations, existing staff, such as IT personnel or co-op students, may be utilized to support the CTI program. However, in most cases, additional personnel will need to be hired, either as full-time employees or contractors, to meet the established intelligence requirements and to ensure the effective operation of the CTI program.

The cost of human capital is often the most significant expense in establishing and running a CTI program. It is essential to have accurate estimates of the required resources to ensure that the program is optimized and cost-effective. A developer can play a significant role in the success of the CTI program by automating tasks, streamlining processes, and reducing the reliance on manual labor. This can optimize the cost of the program and ensure its long-term sustainability.

Human capital is a key component of a CTI program, and organizations must ensure that they have the necessary resources and personnel to support their operations. A thorough analysis of intelligence requirements and carefully considering the cost of human capital and the benefits of automation are crucial to ensuring the success of the CTI program.

Financial Support (Budget)

One of the key factors that contribute to the success of a CTI team is adequate financial support. It is crucial to allocate a comprehensive budget that covers all necessary expenditures to ensure the effective implementation of CTI operations. When planning CTI operations, it is essential to consider the financial requirements and ensure that the budget is sufficient to cover all expenses. A well-funded CTI team is better equipped to carry out its intelligence-gathering activities and achieve its ultimate goals.

The budget for the CTI team should include provisions for hiring the right personnel, as skilled human resources are crucial for effective intelligence gathering. It should also cover the cost of purchasing necessary hardware and software, as technology is critical to intelligence gathering and analysis. Moreover, the budget should encompass funds for subscribing to intelligence services that provide valuable insights to the CTI team.

To optimize the impact of the budget allocated to the CTI team, it is vital to consider the financial requirements when determining the intelligence requirements. This allows the team to estimate the budget and adjust its operations as needed to ensure that resources are used efficiently. If the budget allocated to the CTI team is limited, leadership may request changes to operations and support to reduce costs.

An alternative operating plan in place, such as alternative tools and intelligence sources, will enable the CTI team to meet its intelligence requirements even with a limited budget. This proactive approach helps the team operate effectively and efficiently, even in challenging financial circumstances. By prioritizing adequate financial support and considering financial requirements when planning CTI operations, organizations can increase the effectiveness of their CTI teams and enhance their cyber security posture.

Other executive and stakeholder support

While financial support from executives and stakeholders is important, it's not the only kind of support that is necessary for the success of a Cyber Threat Intelligence (CTI) team. Providing dedicated office space for the team is crucial, allowing them to work without interruptions and operate smoothly. A dedicated workspace designed to meet their unique needs can significantly increase their productivity and effectiveness, which is essential for maintaining a secure environment.

To effectively carry out their duties, the CTI team requires access to various security tools such as Security Information and Event Management (SIEM), Intrusion Detection Systems (IDS), Intrusion Prevention Systems (IPS), and vulnerability scanning tools. The team must have the necessary server and application support to utilize these tools and quickly respond to potential threats.

Other lines of business, such as vulnerability management, information security, finance, and product teams, can provide valuable resources, expertise, and guidance to help the CTI team achieve its goals. Such teams can help the CTI team understand the organization's security posture, identify areas that need improvement, and align with the organization's overall security goals and objectives.

Moreover, supporting the CTI team can also build trust and credibility with executives and stakeholders. When other teams support the CTI team, it demonstrates the organization's commitment to maintaining a secure environment and taking the necessary steps to achieve this. The more support the CTI team has from top to bottom, the more effectively they can integrate with existing teams and carry out their operations, leading to a more efficient and effective CTI team. Ultimately, this is essential for mitigating potential risks and maintaining a secure environment.

Action Items

Begin to plan how you are going to present your proposal for a CTI team to your executives and stakeholders based on all the work efforts you have performed to this point:

- Devise a means to present your ideas on how to defend against cyber threats that can impact your organization and its operations.
  - Typically, this should be in a PowerPoint/slide deck format.
  - Highlight and outline the cyber threat that you are attempting to defend against.
  - Highlight CTI activities, products and services, and mitigation efforts that will defend against cyber-threats.
- Identify how you plan to track and report the activities performed by the CTI team over time.
- During your presentation, your audience may have feedback, and other ideas to incorporate into your overall CTI plan.
- This may include but is not limited to other teams involved in your mitigation activities, changes to intelligence requirements (additions/removals), and operations due to limited resources (human, technology, budgetary).

During your presentation, your executives and stakeholders may have comments that need to be incorporated into your overall plan. This could include new intelligence requirements, an enhancement to the products and services, and alternatives and replacements for some components of the proposed CTI program. This could result in multiple rounds of meetings and updates to ensure that the proposal is in line with the organization's overall security strategy and meets or exceeds the requirements of your executive and stakeholders.

Summary

During this chapter, the focus was developing presentations for executives and stakeholders about intelligence requirements and CTI operations. The goal was to secure "Executive Buy-in" by explaining and clarifying the identified cyber threats and their associated intelligence requirements and presenting proposals on how to identify and defend against these threats. In addition, the objective was to assess, tailor, and update the intelligence requirements based on the feedback received from executives and stakeholders. This involved presenting clear and concise information about the current state of the CTI program, outlining the proposed plans for defending against cyber threats, and seeking input and feedback from those who play critical roles in the organization. The presentations and feedback received would then be used to fine-tune and improve the intelligence requirements, ensuring that they are effective and efficient in meeting the organization's needs.

Now it's your turn to present your Intelligence Requirements and other required operational supports to your organization's executives or other stakeholders to get their buy-in. So get those Intelligence Requirements defined, establish your products and services, explain how you will help defend the organization to cyber threats, and present your plan!

Best of luck in your journey to stand up a Cyber Threat Intelligence program within your organization.

www.ingramcontent.com/pod-product-compliance
Lightning Source LLC
LaVergne TN
LVHW051440050326
832903LV00030BD/3179